YOKED

YOKED

Stories of a Clergy Couple in Marriage, Family, and Ministry

Andrew Kort and Mihee Kim-Kort

An Alban Institute Book

ROWMAN & LITTLEFIELD
Lanham • Boulder • New York • London

Unless otherwise noted, all Scripture quotations are from the New Revised Standard Version of the Bible, copyright © 1989, Division of Christian Education of the National Council of the Churches of Christ in the United States of America, and are used by permission.

Published by Rowman & Littlefield
A wholly owned subsidary of The Rowman & Littlefield Publishing Group, Inc.
4501 Forbes Boulevard, Suite 200, Lanham, Maryland 20706
www.rowman.com

Unit A, Whitacre Mews, 26-34 Stannery Street, London SE11 4AB

British Library Cataloguing in Publication Information Available

Library of Congress Cataloging-in-Publication Data

Kort, Andrew, 1974–
Yoked : stories of a clergy couple in marriage, family, and ministry / Andrew Kort and Mihee Kim-Kort.
pages cm
"An Alban Institute book."
Includes bibliographical references.
ISBN 978-1-56699-764-5 (cloth : alk. paper) — ISBN 978-1-56699-726-3 (pbk. : alk. paper) — ISBN 978-1-56699-727-0 (electronic)
1. Kort, Andrew, 1974– 2. Kim-Kort, Mihee. 3. Clergy couples—United States—Biography. 4. Clergy—United States—Biography. I. Kim-Kort, Mihee. II. Title.
BV675.7.K67 2014
253'.22—dc23
2014022363

Printed in the United States of America

To our parents, who taught us much about ministry, not only in the church but also at home, by being loving parents and modeling a faithful, joyful, and authentic marriage.

CONTENTS

FOREWORD

I have been part of a clergy couple for just shy of thirty years. We have clergy couple friends all over—some serving in the same ministry, some in different placements. For almost fifteen years, I have served at a church where four other staff members are married to clergy people. My congregation sits just down the street from a seminary whose yearly graduating class always includes couples who one day expect to be yoked in ministry. In the mainline Protestant church, clergy couples are no longer treated as novelties. To put it another way, maybe it's time to declare that the shine is officially off clergy couple-hood.

Drawing on decades of experience when it comes to the clergy couple phenomenon, the wider church now knows that a couple yoked in ministry is not a tricky way for a congregation to get two leaders for the price of one. Testimonies abound from couples who point to the challenge of the search process or finding the next call or balancing a two-career relationship. And I will never forget that one Christmas Eve when we had to hire a babysitter for the night. Someone ought to be telling seminarians that the clergy couple life is not as easy as it looks!

So along come Andy Kort and Mihee Kim-Kort, writing not just about the challenge but also about the profound joy, the outright struggle and the deep reward, the ordinary and extraordinary realities of life together as a couple in ministry. Their book reads like a memoir of ministry life, bouncing back and forth between the authors as their respective writing styles so aptly represent each voice. Andy and Mihee's friends will find each chapter to be authentic regarding who they are. Experienced pastors will find their own memories sparked by the stories told and the specifics shared. And, yes, readers who are pondering a life together in ordained ministry will encounter a heartfelt witness to what God may have in store.

With humble spirits, a good dose of humor, and almost uncomfortable honesty, Mihee and Andy invite their readers into their lives. Everyone should be able to find a conversation starter: discerning a call, leadership style in ministry, raising children, finding Sabbath. These topics and others are raised with everyday examples to consider from real experience in life and ministry. An uncommon vulnerability and transparency also allows room for folks who might have made a different decision in a similar situation or the readers who would take a different approach to the complexities of ministry partnership. With a few decades' more experience behind me, I found myself chuckling, sighing, and shaking my head. But everything here resonates with my life in a clergy couple and my life in ministry.

Years ago I sat down for a conversation with Andy early in his ministry, before he and Mihee were married. I remember Andy worrying that the pastor he was then serving with seemed to be working all the time. He wasn't sure he could (or should) try to keep up or take his cues from the older, experienced pastor who had his own seemingly tireless rhythms. The uncertainty quickly spread to a question about fitness for ministry in general and whether Andy was cut out for this vocational life.

We had a sort of "aha" moment when I reminded him that the accountants and business school graduates his age just starting out were going to and from their offices every day with the person in the corner office there before they arrived and still there when they left. Some of the very real challenges we face are not unique to ministry in the parish setting. I think of that conversation and that "aha" moment because I think this book easily translates to couples everywhere trying to find wisdom, follow a call, and experience a meaning-filled life together. One can imagine a book group in the congregation enjoying the reading and the conversation that follows. Lay folks will surprised about how much they have to contribute from their own lives. At the very least, a congregation can get a behind-the-scenes look at highs and lows of life when two pastors are married.

The shine may be off when it comes to clergy couples. And, yes, it is harder than anyone is willing to say. But from one member of clergy couple who has been blessed to thrive in my marriage and my ministry, I am grateful to Mihee and Andy for having the vision and the heart to lead us all in a conversation.

David A. Davis
Nassau Presbyterian Church
Princeton, New Jersey

ACKNOWLEDGMENTS

The word *acknowledgment* certainly does not do justice to the gratitude we feel toward so many who have been a part of this journey. There are people who have yoked themselves to us in so many ways. They prayed for us. They listened to us. They encouraged us. They were our lifelines not only in times of change and transition but also in those ordinary seasons. They modeled community and ministry, life together, in rich ways to us. We are where and who we are because of their faithfulness to the Good, and how they have been Christ to us in countless circumstances.

Thank you to all those at Alban—who worked on a difficult manuscript with painstaking care and attention—and particularly to Fritz Gutwein for his patience and presence.

ANDY KORT

I give thanks for the kindness, grace, and friendship of mentors and colleagues in ministry, and especially for Dave and Cathy Davis and Bill Crawford and Julie Parker, two of our earliest and best models of a clergy couple working and living together. Their wisdom along the way has been amazing and invaluable.

For Dennis Jones and Burns Stanfield, who have been beyond supportive, encouraging, and inspiring throughout the years. For seminary professors and leaders Brian Blount, Patrick Miller, John Obrien-Prager, and especially Bob Jacks, who were formative for me while at Princeton and continue to stimulate and encourage me today.

For Jay Bowers, Colin Yuckman, Matt Gough, Katie and Robby Crowe, Jeff Bryan, Alex Wimberly, Scott Hauser, Charlie Dupree, and Jonas Hayes. You are all my best friends in life and in ministry, and I love you dearly.

For the church communities I have served and, especially, for the members and staff at First Presbyterian Church of Bloomington, Indiana. You all make ministry a joy and have ministered to our family in unbelievable ways.

For my grandmother, Pauline Kort, who wanted to be a missionary but answered the call to raise a wonderful family instead. Thank you for praying and singing hymns with me. For the life of my grandfather, Robert Closson. Serving communion to him around a simple kitchen table in Portland, Maine, on one of our last visits together continues to be a profound reminder of the power of God.

For my parents, Tom and Corrine Kort, and my sister, Sarah. You continue to remind me that I am a son, brother, and beloved child of God. And, of course, for Mihee, Desmond, Anna, and Oswald. You are God's most amazing gifts to my life. All of you are answered prayers.

MIHEE KIM-KORT

I echo much of what Andy is thankful for throughout this process, and in our journey together. I have to lift up again the conversations with Erica Liu, Kiran Wimberley, Christine Hong, Grace Ji-Sun Kim, and Lauren Joujan. Somehow they helped me make sense of my rambling thoughts, and even affirmed them. My parents and brother and sister-in-law are a never-ending source of support. Emma Moore, a college student, but a wise, old soul beyond her years, and my anchor of sanity, provided numerous hours of babysitting so that I could put down a few words on paper. The church community of First Presbyterian–Bloomington has been our extended family in town. My new moms group—the key to my survival these last three years—Christie, Kristine, Kristi, Kate, Katie, Meg, Tiff, and Ashley—has toiled with me in this endeavor called motherhood, rejoiced with me during my second pregnancy, and served as the embodiment of gracious and loving community.

And finally, last but not least, Andy, Desmond, Anna, and Oswald, you continue to be my muse—inspiring me toward love and good deeds for the sake of God's kingdom.

This project began shortly after the twins were born and we moved to Bloomington, Indiana, for our new call in ministry and life together. We had no idea how much the process would change us, and the gratitude we have toward God is difficult to measure in human terms. It is such a privilege to be able to share our story with you, so thank you, dear readers, for giving this work a chance, too.

INTRODUCTION

As we were about to embark on the twofold adventure of ordained ministry and marriage, we were given a lot of advice. Or rather, we were given a lot of commentary. Many of our friends were thrilled and shared in our excitement, as we were all set to plow ahead into these two callings. We were going to change the world! Or so we thought. Others, who were wiser and married, and especially those who were in this unique situation of being a "clergy couple," simply smiled knowingly and said, "Good luck."

Looking back, we wish we had taken more time to sit and listen to these clergy couple veterans who had the scars to prove their mettle, the wisdom to shed light on some of what was headed our way, and the grace to encourage two newlyweds on the track to ordination. But we didn't, because we thought we knew it all already. Or, if we did listen once in a while, we thought, "Surely, that can't or won't be us."

Ten years into this life together, we looked back and wondered about some of the experiences and hardship, all the questions that we didn't even think to ask anyone. We wondered what it would have been like to read something that would have named some of those challenges for us and helped us verbalize those questions. We wondered what it would have been like if more churches understood what it means to hire a pastor who is married to a pastor, and how it isn't easy to negotiate the expectations of two communities.

We looked for resources. As it turns out, there is not a surplus pertaining to clergy couples. Looking for some statistics or information, Andy called the Pew Research Center. According to its website, "Pew Research Center is a nonpartisan fact tank that informs the public about the issues, attitudes and trends shaping America and the world." Surely they would have something. He was passed around a few times and finally landed in the religion department. They had nothing on clergy couples. When Andy said he was looking for statistics or any research on clergy couples, he was told, "This is the first time we've been asked about that. Sorry to not be of more help to you."

We were also able to find a document called "Clergy Couples Guidance" by the Church of England,[1] but this seems to be more of a resource for churches to navigate having a clergy couple on staff. We were also happy to discover that later this year, 2014, a camp and conference center is hosting a conference for couples in ministry. Curiously to us, this camp and conference center is affiliated with our denomination, PC (USA), and yet only by digging online did we come across this resource. We have yet to see or hear anything about it otherwise. A final result of our online search yielded the only book that we could find on the subject of clergy couples, and it has to do with crisis.[2] Granted, clergy couples are a rare phenomenon, but they are not as rare as they used to be. We were surprised by the lack of resources and material dedicated to them.

Turning to an online search, we found an article through Duke Divinity School titled "Wedded to the Future: Clergy Couples Provide a New Paradigm for Leadership."[3] It is a good article that mentions some of the issues we write about: family, models, and compromise. At the end, a ten-point "Clergy Couple Survival Guide" is offered. Elsewhere online, we found a *Ministry* magazine article about clergy couples and counseling. It highlights particular needs of, and eight common issues among, clergy couples.[4] In another search, we were able to find some information that mentioned clergy couples, but it fit into the larger context of other issues. For instance, in his book *The Church: Sacraments, Worship, Ministry, Mission*, Donald G. Bloesch mentions a "disturbingly high divorce rate for clergy couples."[5] However, we were unable to find any hard statistics as to what that rate is, especially compared to others. Interestingly, in *Clergy Women: An Uphill Calling*, the authors were also curious to see if clergy couples divorced more or less frequently than other clergy. They write, "Nonetheless, no evidence exists that marrying a person who is ordained will result in a greater likelihood of divorce for a clergy woman or a clergy man." They go on to say, "For ordained women and men married to other clergy, numerous factors in their lives and personalities create or exacerbate the conflicts in their marriages that lead to divorce."[6]

Bottom line: There are too few resources. A quick search on Google for "books on clergy couples" could actually lead one to believe that clergy couples are only in crisis.

And so we wanted to share some of our stories—all the successes and failures, all the trial-by-error, fly-by-the-seat-of-our-pants methods, all the reflections we've come to when we've had time and brain cells—for whatever they are worth. If nothing else, our hope is this volume will bear witness to the reality that, while extraordinarily challenging at times, the work and life of a clergy couple can and does yield much good fruit, along with a lot of joy. Truly, there is joy, and there are moments when we feel like we are flourishing and not just surviving, when we are thriving and not skimming the surface of life—and not only as pastors but also as people.

We have too often found (and we are guilty of this ourselves) that when clergy get together they gripe and complain about everything from the congregation they serve to their feelings of being underpaid and underappreciated, to the frustration of dealing with the mind-numbing amount of administration and emails. Many will say, "This is not what I had in mind when I answered God's call." The same can sometimes be said about marriage: "This is not what I had in mind when I said, 'I do.'" We hope that this book in some way will give voice to the joy of ministry. Looking down at our wedding rings, we are proud of the scratches and dents that they have picked up along the way. These are scars that prove our mettle. It's not always easy or fun, but it often is joyful. And we've found it to be so yoked together, as we are yoked to God.

We are by no means experts, and we would never presume to offer any kind of blueprint or design for success. This could never be an exhaustive study or reflection of even our own lives. Admittedly, we were *exhausted* throughout the two years it took to write this together, because we went from new parents with twins to a surprise pregnancy, and then to three kids under three years of age. All this with two cats (who now live with Pap and Gram) and a dog named Ellis (whom we gradually pushed to the very bottom of the totem pole). We were in a new town, at a new church, and negotiating other commitments, like serving on committees and boards. Not to mention trying to squeeze in some sleep here and there. So much of it is raw, and may even seem incomplete, as if we were right in the middle of figuring something out.

In spite of it all, we believe that we have some wisdom to share from our experiences thus far, both in marriage and in ministry. Namely, ways to do life, and ways *not* to do it—in other words, please learn from our mistakes and failures. We certainly have no shame about most of it, and we hope that it provides some encouragement.

A brief note about the reflections and questions at the end of the chapters: They are written assuming the reader is in a clergy couple. After all, we can only speak from our own particular experience and would never presume to impose our experiences on anyone. However, we do hope that they may be applicable in some way to all who share this call to God's service.

Andy Kort
Mihee Kim-Kort

I

COLLISION

Sharing Dreams and Calling

MIHEE KIM-KORT

> God, Who enlightens the minds and inflames the hearts of the faithful
> by the Holy Spirit, grant that through the same Spirit I may know my
> true vocation in life, and may have the grace to follow it faithfully.
> Through Christ our Lord, Amen.
>
> —Catholic Vocation Prayer

> I am ultimately one who is willing to walk and to work with a dream
> announced of old in the words of Genesis, and brought to bear in the
> poetry and prose of people of color the world over: "Behold, the
> Dreamer cometh" (Gn. 37:19). I have a dream that womanists, muje-
> ristas, and feminists can appropriate one another's work with integrity,
> and with true reciprocity . . . I have a dream that the tables can overlap,
> that they must overlap—that the table of professionalism and the nour-
> ishment of academe must serve and become a table of solidarity and
> community for all those who are oppressed through lack of knowl-
> edge, or lack of empowerment in mind and in body.
>
> —Toinette M. Eugene in *Feminist Theological Ethics: A Reader* [1]

My mother had dreams for me.

These days, though, when my mother, now in her late fifties, *has* night
dreams about me and my younger brother, she tells me that in her dreams
we are always children, even though *we're in our thirties*. She says some-

times we are running down the small hill in a backyard, or we are sitting at the old kitchen table with our feet swinging high above the floors and our heads barely above the surface. Sometimes we are sitting in front of the television or reading a book on the couch talking in high-pitched cartoony voices. Sometimes we are in a car together driving somewhere, and I'm sitting in the back asking her questions. My mother tells me these dreams with a misty-eyed wistfulness. She never fails to remind me that we are still her babies.

When I was a child, both of my parents had other dreams of us on a regular basis. They would tell us that it was because we were always on their minds, day and night. But they also had dreams *for* me. Those dreams, they would tell me, led them across oceans and continents, to this place, this land of "endless opportunity" away from everything familiar and comfortable. For me, they were dreams about wealth and success, power and influence, accomplishment and fame, and, most of all, dreams of a professional vocation that would require years at a top-notch school. Somehow, those dreams permeated my own night dreams, and my daydreams, too. And while their unspoken dreams for themselves shifted as my father went to seminary late in life, I found mine changing as well.

It was not meant to be an easy conversation when I shared how they were shifting to something altogether different.

Ambition: Their Dreams for Me

> Without leaps of imagination, or dreaming, we lose the excitement of possibilities. Dreaming, after all, is a form of planning.
> —Gloria Steinem[2]

When I was finishing up my first year in college, I expressed a desire to explore pursuing full-time ministry. I remember my mother sat quietly, pursing her lips. I asked her what she thought about it, and she replied with questions:

"How will you be a mother?"
"How will you be a wife and take care of your husband?"
"Do you know how hard ministry is on a person?"

My shoulders sagged a little as I listened to every question heavy with uncertainty, every worry and anxiety coloring her voice. I couldn't help but wonder how she would have expected me to accomplish all this while being a doctor or lawyer—yet I kept the question to myself. "It's just something I'm thinking about right now."

I tried to make light of this season of discernment. She didn't really buy it. As my ambitions turned toward preparing for seminary and continuing on in religion classes, I felt a wall growing between us. Fortunately, it was temporary.

I realize now that her dreams were always for me to be, first, healthy; second, happy; and third, a wife and a mother. Pretty simple and straightforward. Now that I am on the other side of seminary and marriage and a family, with twins who are toddlers, and another on the way, I can see a little of why she worried, and why she always hoped this for me. *What seems like a small ambition is actually often the best dream—health and happiness.* And yet, while she hopes for this simple thing for me, she realizes that part of this dream means enjoying and thriving in ministry. She dreams that I will make a positive impact on the world that our babies are growing up in right now and will eventually inherit from us.

It took some time to get to this place. I had dreams of my own, but my mother's dreams mattered to me, too. When they finally overlapped, I can't pinpoint the exact moment, but that they were her dreams, and her dreams were mine, holds some significance in my vocational identity. But I never expected the road. Plans often get waylaid in my life, and this was no exception.

When I met Andy, I had no dreams of relationships, long-term commitments, and, certainly, family at the time. I had gone to seminary with one goal in mind. I wanted to be an ordained minister and care for Korean American youth in a church. I loved the church I grew up in, and realized in college that I wanted to facilitate community in a similar way for other Korean American youth. This seemed so vitally important to me at the time, even if I couldn't totally articulate this call. No doubt, though, the seeds of ministry were planted in so many ways and nurtured by conversations with staff, pastors, and other leaders. I was navigating college courses and attending all sorts of gatherings for various Christian fellowships. And I began thinking about seminary, not coincidentally at the same time my father began full-time studies.

My conversation with him was quite different from my mother's. It was my father—the ultimate symbol of Asian patriarchy—who would make the biggest impact on me concerning ministry. When I started my undergraduate studies, I had planned on going pre-med and took too many science classes at once. But I fell in love with the humanities courses. I would never have considered actually pursuing ordained ministry in a million years until that one conversation late at night. My father was attending Princeton Seminary at the time and enjoying the classes and community with numerous women who were studying to also become . . . ordained ministers.

"Ministers??? You mean, preaching in the pulpit??? But the Bible says that women are supposed to submit to men—and church leaders are supposed to only be men; I can't imagine a woman being able to do it! That just sounds wrong."

I argued with him over the phone, and we went back and forth.

With conviction, he told me stories of how women had been leaders of the church for a long time, and many were elders in the Presbyterian Church, and also becoming pastors all around him—they had a voice. And he admired and respected them and, in fact, supported them. He reminded me that the first people to preach the gospel after Jesus's resurrection were women. He was even taking a class on feminist/womanist theologies—the same class that would impact me deeply some years later during my own seminary coursework.

Later, I would encounter Serene Jones, author of *Feminist Theory and Christian Theology*. She tells the story of sitting on a search committee that was debating whether a woman should be called as the church's next pastor. Some members said women are more nurturing than men, and therefore more pastoral and better listeners. Some thought a woman minister would be better with the children in the congregation. Others argued that having a woman as a minister would make a difference in a negative way, although they couldn't really articulate how; one member said, "It's just not the same."[3]

And I started to have a glimpse of the kind of struggle I would face in pursuing this vocation. But I knew I wouldn't be alone. My father encouraged me: "And you can be a leader, too, an elder, a pastor, anything you believe God is calling you to be in your own life," he said to me. "*God can speak to you through your dreams. Sometimes those dreams will surprise you.* But don't let anyone tell you what you can or cannot do for God's kingdom."

Though my parents had initially different responses, their dreams widened to include mine, but they ultimately wanted one thing: for me to live and work faithfully and happily. I couldn't imagine a better way to live my life.

Anticipation: My Dreams for Me

> The real shortage we face is dreams, and the wherewithal and the will to make them come true.
>
> —Seth Godin[4]

It was a turning point. When I finally stepped into the same classrooms my father had been in a few short years before, instead of ambition, it was anticipation that carried me forward. Expectation. Hope. The possibilities seemed endless, and while the classes challenged all my core beliefs, and thus my core self, it was a change I felt was right. It was the right season.

Still, it wasn't easy, and those long-held beliefs did not go quietly into the night: *What do you mean Moses didn't write the first five books of the Bible? What do you mean we can't just pray away mental disease? What do you mean the flood likely didn't happen or Mary wasn't a virgin?*

Strangely enough, even though everything seemed to be unraveling for me, I found my experience of God growing and expanding in ways that were inexplicable, and yet more tangible than anything in my journey so far. Though I discovered far more questions, and learned to let go of black-and-white answers, it seemed a much more faithful way to live out my faith. And this spilled out onto my calling as well. *The less sure I became about where God would lead me, the more I lived with anticipation of how that call would surface each day, and, most of all, I became more certain of God's faithfulness and partnership with me in this journey.* I could serve anywhere God called me, whether a Korean American church or abroad. All I knew was that the call process wouldn't end with graduation.

But, early on during my seminary career, my life took an even stranger turn.

The first weekend of summer language, I met a second year student—Andy. We were hanging out in a large group in one of the dorms getting ready to go out. He was wearing a black T-shirt, jeans, and a Pirates hat on backward. Tall and quiet, I couldn't help but be drawn to him a little. We didn't talk much that first night, but afterward we began to spend time together—adventures in NYC, late night runs to Hoagie Haven, and study sessions. Now, if someone would have told me about Andy and what he would become in my life that first week during Hebrew Summer Language, I would have said, "What do you mean I'll meet the man who would eventually become my husband? What do you mean I'm going to end up a *sa-moh-nim* [pastor's wife]?"

I revolted. Andy and I would go on to date for about a year, which in seminary terms actually means ten years. It was an intense year, struggling with this sense of call shifting in my life to make space for the possibility of a long-term commitment in so many spheres of my life. I felt I wasn't ready—for any of it—so I did what made sense at the time. I ran. We broke up the summer between my first and second year. I needed to find myself. And I did, in a way, and it was in connection to Andy. Later that year, we got back together, we were engaged shortly after, and married less than a year later. The rest is, as they say, history.

Transformation: God's Dreams for Me

The new expectation I began to embrace was that any and all my expectations were fair game, and that I should prepare for them to be blown sky-high in this new season. I never thought I would have married the man of my dreams during seminary. It certainly wasn't a fairy-tale-happily-ever-after right away, as we struggled to adjust to each other, and especially to each other's callings. I was approaching my graduation and, like many other seniors, interviewing for positions at local churches. Every position seemed like the perfect possibility, and I felt so affirmed in my calling. But it wasn't meant to be for me. At least, not yet.

So, in fact, it seemed like a mess at the time, but when I look back now, I can't imagine it happening any other way. My dreams had collided with Andy's dreams, but in a way, it was a glimpse into God's dreams for us, and the result was more miraculous than I ever thought possible. What God did with me in the midst of this shifting was more than help me adjust my timeline. It was an adjustment of my vision.

> For surely I know the plans I have for you, says the Lord, plans for your welfare and not for harm, to give you a future with hope. Then when you call upon me and come and pray to me, I will hear you. When you search for me, you will find me; if you seek me with all your heart, I will let you find me, says the Lord. (Jeremiah 29:11–14a)

And I can still say that with total confidence even now.

After my graduation, I moved up to Mamaroneck, New York, to the manse for the associate pastor of Larchmont Avenue Church, where Andy had somehow managed to live the past year during the weeks, with only a mattress on the floor, a few dishes and silverware, and a radio. Even though I had no idea where I would end up in ministry, I felt I had come home. Andy was there.

> When the Lord restored the fortunes of Zion, we were like those who dream. Then our mouth was filled with laughter, and our tongue with shouts of joy; then it was said among the nations, "The Lord has done great things for them." The Lord has done great things for us, and we rejoiced. (Psalm 126)

Although I ended up working at Starbucks and doing other odd jobs like substitute teaching, it was a useful year. We enjoyed our married life as much as possible, and we often dreamed aloud together about the future. We dreamed of churches and children, mission trips and ministry. We had some tumultuous times, too, as I floundered and thrashed my way through those questions of *what would be in store for me* and *how long would it take to get there.* There were a lot of tears. Late nights wrestling with a profound angst. And shouting.

Thankfully, we found someone to talk to together. We went to a marriage counselor who was also a clergy person and understood what it meant to work in a church. She didn't solve our problems. She didn't help us make any future plans. She didn't help us with our callings. But the best thing she did for us was help us connect to each other more. She helped us to see how we needed to communicate with one another, so that we were truly supportive and yoked together in a way that would be foundational to the rest of our lives. After we moved, we continued to be in contact with another, older clergy couple from the seminary, and hearing their own process gave us tangible help. We learned through all of this that our partnership would be what sustains us in our callings, and in the process of living into our dreams and callings together.

Most importantly, those dreams that kept me up at all hours were not experienced in isolation, and I can say with all honesty and gratitude that Andy helped me to fill both my days and my nights. And I did eventually find myself on the other side, but only to find that there was so much more to come.

ANDY KORT

> Yes: I am a dreamer. For a dreamer is one who can only find his way
> by moonlight, and his punishment is that he sees the dawn before the
> rest of the world.
>
> —Oscar Wilde[5]

Understanding calling—it is one of the great mysteries of our life of faith.
Namely, how do we decipher, determine, and discern what it is God is
"calling" us to do? And how do we know how much of this is what God
wants us to do and how much of it is our own desires bubbling to the top
like the gurgling boil over a hot cauldron? Does God only call us to one
thing at a time? And, let's be honest, what's the difference between a call
and a job, especially for someone who is just finishing up graduate school
and excited about applying their developing skills to the trade? These are
not easy questions. We struggled with these questions when I began my
first call. Mihee's first "call" after seminary was working as a barista at
Starbucks, and it was incredibly hard to live out this season when we had
both graduated from the same school with the same degree, and the same
readiness for ministry, but only one of us was in the church. I suffered
and agonized with her as she sought to understand God's timing for her
and me. What did it mean that God was calling her to one place, and
myself to another, and how could we support each other's work in God's
kingdom?

God's calling. I wrestle with the strange reality that God calls us—
human beings—to do his work in the world. And why some now and not
others, like Mihee who was equally capable and called to ministry, creative and energetic, and who overcame much to get there? Why some now,
like me who had a different journey toward ministry and wanted something completely different in the beginning?

Maybe it's the Calvin fanatic in me talking, but part of my understanding of who we are as humans leads me to believe that we are more than
just a little bit selfish. If given a choice, like the Apostle Paul, we do what
we know we shouldn't be doing at any given moment. Maybe we even
talk ourselves into doing what we want by convincing ourselves that what
we want is probably what God wants for us. I think we see this all over
the Old Testament, starting with Adam and Eve, who may have done this
in the Garden. In what might be the first calling in the Bible, God wanted
Eve and Adam to simply stay away from the fruit of the tree of knowl-

edge. They were called to attend to the fruit of the other trees, plants, bushes, the animals, birds of the air, and things that creep and crawl. God had given them dominion over these things. They were to care for and oversee them. That was their calling. But did they listen to it? Of course not. They did what they wanted to do for themselves. And they rationalized it. They spun it so that it seemed like it wouldn't be that big of a deal: *Surely, God as our Creator would understand our desires. God being in relationships with us, God would want us to be happy, right?*

Being Called In: God's Desire for Relationship

I thought *I knew* what I would need to do to be happy. Even with my call to ministry, I had plans for how that journey would pan out.

At the time I was in seminary, I honestly believed that my calling rested somewhere within the realm of ministry in the local church. Leading up to seminary, I had some pivotal experiences as a volunteer leader on two mission trips, one to Mexico and one to the mountains of North Carolina. These moments helped confirm the sense of call that I was wrestling with at the time. I also helped with the senior high youth group on Sunday nights. I got to know the youth. We talked easily. We sat next to each other in worship. We went to movies and to get ice cream. They wrapped my car in toilet paper. I was engaged in ministry for the first time. I was discovering the joy of community, and the relationships within the community expressed God's love for me in new ways. I felt fully alive and I loved it.

As my seminary career began, I immediately fell deeper in love with it all. The Greek, the theology, the intro classes, my new friends, and even New Jersey. I took some great classes with some amazing professors who were able to knock me for a theological loop. I heard sermons that were homiletical humdingers. Certainly, there were lectures that could cure insomnia, but that is part of the experience, and part of the fun. As my schedule allowed me to take electives, I took several youth ministry courses. Working with youth was where I had experience. It was where I had confidence. It was what I thought I enjoyed the most. It was what I thought would make me happy. I thought God was, at the time, calling me to pursue youth ministry.

It was then that I started taking more theology courses, preaching courses, pastoral care courses, and worship courses. During that time, I also fulfilled the required "field education" internships. I respected and admired my classmates who took assignments outside of their zones of comfort, to try some new experiences, although, like many of my classmates, I went to work in a small church nearby doing mostly, yes, youth ministry.

But I also got to teach, preach, lead worship, and visit with families. And I discovered, "This is it." This is what drew me in. I couldn't believe how much I loved it. While I still loved and cared for youth, I felt God shaping in me an openness to a different possibility. *It was an adjustment to realize that I didn't need to feel confident about my ability. That wasn't the basis of my call. At that time, what I needed were a listening ear and a willing heart.*

More importantly, this was what spoke to me the most about God's grace, and God's desire to love, care for, and be in relationship with humanity. Sure, I was in the familiar setting of the local church, but like my classmates who were doing clinical pastoral education or organizing community soup kitchens, I was stretched and doing something that was not only brand new for me but also fresh in terms of seeing God at work in the lives of others, and especially in my own life. When I registered for classes again, my days of taking youth ministry courses were over. Now, for the very first time, I saw myself as someone God might actually be able to use to help lead a congregation.

In this shift, I realized that calling wasn't about pursuing my own personal ideas of happiness, but being drawn into God's love in new ways and discovering that grace in all the relationships I was building in the church community, with youth and adults, children and grandparents. God was changing me, not only my sense of calling but also our own relationship, as well as my faith.

Being Called Together: God's Desire for Commitment

A vision is not just a picture of what could be; it is an appeal to our better selves, a call to become something more.
—Rosabeth Moss Kanter, Harvard Business School professor[6]

Somewhere during that year I met Mihee. Actually, it was in July as we were taking the intensive summer Hebrew course. There are various versions abounding of the story of what happened next. But my spin on the story is that this girl just would not leave me alone. And truth be told, I wouldn't leave her alone. There were butterflies, laughs, joys, fights, disagreements, and a few short-lived breakups. If you go by the odds and percentages compiled by people who keep track of these things, Mihee and I have no business being together. Or, at least, the relationship was destined to be doomed.

We are both the oldest sibling in our families. We are both very stubborn. We are an inter-racial couple. We are a clergy couple in a vocational field where you can't always just simply roll into town and get a job, like the businessperson, engineer, or telecommuting consultant. There is an almost five-year age difference. She identifies with the West Coast, and I identify with the East Coast. She is laid back, and I am not. She grew up much more conservative than me. Her parents, initially, were not thrilled with the idea of me. She was raised in a traditional Korean home, and at the time I couldn't even use chopsticks. The more all of these things collided into the relationship and the story that is Mihee and me, the more convinced I became that this relationship is in its own way a calling. It is only by the grace of God that each morning we wake up and answer that call with another "yes."

I was, in seminary terms, a year ahead of Mihee. As my senior year reached its midway point, we were forced to make some serious decisions about our relationship, our life together, our calls—as we then understood them—and what might happen to us. We wanted similar things and had similar visions. It was impossibly hard to imagine life without the other. But there were pragmatic challenges to think through for our life together. She had a year of seminary left. How would we figure this out? I was about to graduate from a very well-respected seminary, and I was ready to receive a call to ministry. I was eager to jump right into full-time ministry. I certainly didn't want to work at Barnes & Noble while she finished her degree. I could also kiss the dream of a semester with golf, beer, and books in Scotland goodbye. But that dream would not even be close to being the last one bound to the altar and sacrificed as we listened for God's call.

In a leap of faith, I bought a ring with a princess cut diamond on the top. On the Princeton Battlefield one evening, I gave it to her. She laughed for a long time before saying yes.

But we still had a lot to figure out. I compiled my dossier and sent it to churches that were in commuting distance to Princeton. Even though I

felt more and more called to the ministry of Word and Sacrament, I didn't
think I was ready—or mature—enough to be a solo pastor. I felt I needed
to be mentored by someone who would teach me how to run meetings,
give me space to make mistakes, and grow professionally before I'd go at
it on my own. Like Moses, I didn't think I was up for a big job like
leading a flock all by myself. Of course, I could have done it. I see that
much more clearly now.

Shortly after my graduation, a call came from an amazing church in
Larchmont, New York, a bedroom community just outside of New York
City. The call was for an associate pastor who would focus on youth. It
seemed perfect. I had a great head of staff (and I didn't realize how lucky
I was, or how important that is, until later). I had fantastic co-workers.
The community was gorgeous. The church had much going for it, includ-
ing great families and some pretty incredible youth. Plus, it was a short
train ride, twenty-one miles, into Grand Central Station, and like the
T-shirt proclaims, "I Heart NY."

But I soon found out it was too long of a commute. The back and forth
to Princeton on a daily basis was probably doable, but with many nightly
meetings, the schedule of someone who works with youth, and the price
of gas, it was way too much. So, for almost the first year of our marriage,
we saw each other on the weekends. My call came with an apartment, and
Mihee was in married student housing on campus. Friday was my day off,
and I'd drive down after work on Thursday, arriving late. I'd leave some-
time on Saturday to get back and get ready for worship on Sunday. When
I got "home" to Princeton, I was off and ready to have fun. She still had
exams, papers, and books to read. The fact that I was there didn't change
her professors' due dates. I wanted to play. She needed to work. It was
very hard. Let's just say, we crammed in a week's worth of loving and
fighting into those forty-eight hours. I do not recommend starting out
married life in this way. We survived only because there was a light at the
end of that tunnel: she would graduate in May. We just had to make it
until then, and finally we'd be together as a married couple.

All that being said, looking back, the distance was somewhat of a
good thing. I was able to focus on my ministry and be present in the New
York community without the feeling of "having to get home." She was
able to finish her classes and especially her senior thesis without me
around to bug and distract her. But this season was just the beginning of

learning how to juggle this thing we call God's call. I got my feet wet but didn't realize there was a storm up ahead.

Being Called Out: God's Desire for Partnership

As Mihee's graduation loomed on the horizon, she had many of the same feelings I had just a year earlier. Namely, she had just gone through three years of seminary, and she was ready for a call. She also did not want to work at Barnes & Noble. There was a potential call in suburban Philadelphia, but I had just started in Larchmont. We did briefly consider leaving New York and going to Philly. My head of staff was even supportive. He's in a clergy couple, too, and understands the unique demands. Eventually, we decided I should stay in New York and that she'd join me. I'm glad to report she did not have to work at the local Barnes & Noble. She was spared that. It was Starbucks where she drew her first paycheck with her newly minted Master of Divinity degree. More than just Scotland was on the sacrificial altar, and Scotland now seems like a small loss to bemoan compared to what Mihee gave up for the moment.

In this, she helped me understand a great and profound reality and truth. God's call to us is most often not what we want, would like, or imagine for ourselves. It certainly is not easy. Sacrifices have to be made for it. Often someone gets let down—sometimes it is the pastor who is yoked to another and sometimes a congregation when a pastor is called elsewhere. In this case, it was Mihee who took on that burden and put off being able to receive a call. Not because she wasn't a viable candidate. Not because she was not being faithful. If anything, she *was* being faithful—to me. And by doing so, I believe she was faithful to God. She did so because she loves me that much. She helped me see and understand that before either of us received a call to ordained ministry, we were called to each other in marriage. We respect that. And I think God respects that.

But we are not just yoked together as husband and wife. We are also yoked to God. Someone gave us a wedding gift that had three branches woven together and underneath is the inscription from Ecclesiastes 4:12: "A cord of three is not easily broken." But sometimes that means that one of the three (most often one of the human cords) has to make some significant sacrifices.

Like some of the more well-known call stories in the Bible, sometimes we are called (or one of us is called) to where we do not necessarily want to go and to do what we would rather not really do on any given day. Jonah said, "Anywhere but Nineveh." Moses tried his best to get out of his call: "I can't do it. I can't even talk in public. Isn't there someone else, God, you could call?" Not everyone gets up and sings with gusto "Here I am, Lord." In fact, I know some people who are really sick of that hymn.

But, nevertheless, God calls. God calls people. And people go. They trust, they risk, they try to be faithful, they sacrifice dreams (or at least delay them), they go to Nineveh, they confront the Pharaoh, they move with their husband to New York.

In all of the call stories in the Bible that I can currently think of, it seems to eventually work out. Even if Moses doesn't get to cross the Jordan, he still gets to see it. I wish it was like that for all of us. But I know it is not. Some very honest and faithful people end up in unhealthy situations. They get bitter, burned out, and frustrated; worst of all, they give up on ministry. It's sad. I have to trust that God is even somehow still in that.

And that is the risk in following God's call, however you decide to define, decipher, and discern it. There is an element of unknown danger. We are called into the wilderness, sometimes with others, sometimes alone. And it can be scary. We can end up in a bad situation even though we had all of the best intentions. It's risky. It's not safe to follow God's call. And that might be what makes a call different than a job. It's not about the paycheck or the rung on the ladder. It's about taking a big giant step out in faith, with faith, because for reasons known only to God, we seek to do the Lord's work.

Faith never knows where it is being led, but it loves and knows the One who is leading.

—Oswald Chambers[7]

But it can also be beautiful. Often people today wonder where are all the miracles—"Do they still happen?" they will ask me. If you ask me, a miracle happens whenever a disciple drops their nets and leaves familiarity, family, and friends behind. A miracle happens when someone packs up all of their belongings into the back of a truck or U-Haul and heads to a far-off and distant land, while gripping keys to the manse in one hand and the steering wheel in the other. A miracle happens when those who are equally, if not more, equipped are willing to pull shots of espresso, so their loved one can live into his first call. My understanding of call is not just between me and whatever church I happen to be serving at the moment. To be sure, it includes that. But my understanding of call also has do to with Mihee, and now our two children, and soon to be three. I'm in this with them. And they are in it with me. No matter what the time or what the season, we are a family. We are even a little community. We are yoked. Thanks be to God.

AFTERWORDS

Certainly, our own hopes and dreams for our life, not to mention the dreams of others for us, can be complicated. Having your hopes, dreams, and understanding of God's call on your life collide with another person's, whether they be clergy or not, can be messy. That is usually what happens after a collision. There is often debris to clean up, pieces to put back together, and if humans are involved, there are wounds that need balm. Sometimes one person's hopes and dreams have to change, and often both end up being realized in a much different way. What made sense at one point may no longer be a good or attractive option. As we grow and change, with new experiences, and find ourselves in new situations and circumstances in life, we have to make adjustments. Open and honest conversations, dialogues, and prayers with ourselves, others, and God are crucial. Of course, listening is just as important in those exchanges as talking, if not more. If you are in a relationship, clergy couple or otherwise, taking time to reflect on your own calling and listening to the hopes of the other is vital. Surely, there will be some overlap. Likely, there will be some forks in the road where your ideal paths will diverge in different directions. Being aware and attentive to the hopes, dreams, and callings as well as any changes in them is critical.

—AK

CONNECT

- In what ways have your dreams for ministry veered away from each other?
- How have you defined calling in relationship to one another?
- How are decisions, sacrifices, and adjustments made in your life together?
- In what ways have you discovered your callings overlap?

2

CLOUT

Living into One's Unique Authority and Voice

ANDY KORT

> Discovering vocation does not mean scrambling toward some prize just beyond my reach but accepting the treasure of true self I already possess. Vocation does not come from a voice *out there* calling me to be something I am not. It comes from a voice *in here* calling me to be the person I was born to be, to fulfill the original selfhood given me at birth by God.
>
> —Thomas Merton (emphasis mine)[1]

We have all been shaped and influenced by people who have come into our lives. Thankfully, some have been more influential than others. During the early 1990s as a high school student in Charlotte, North Carolina, I somehow found myself on the varsity basketball team. I'd like to say that I was influenced by someone like Michael Jordan. I would even settle for my personal favorite at the time, Charlotte Hornets forward Larry Johnson. But, as the box scores in the *Charlotte Observer* would show, it appears I was more influenced by Ollie, the small and overmatched player who rarely left the bench in the movie *Hoosiers*. Let's just say I got a lot of splinters.

As is also typical of a teenager, I was influenced by my friends and peers—for better and sometimes for worse. My paternal grandmother and maternal grandfather also have heavily influenced me. I realize this now, more than I ever thought during all the years of visits and monkey business. My grandma taught me about laughter, joy, as well as love of family and God. Actually, she also still influences our family's menu as I make my version of "Grandma's homemade chicken noodle soup" as often as I can get away with it. It's a huge part of why I love cold weather. My grandfather influenced me in the way of humor and love of stories, but also in the desire to stand up for what is right. I think I may have his temper, too.

As should be the case when churches live out their baptismal promises to provide for a child's spiritual growth, many others have nurtured me in my journey of faith. I think of those who taught Sunday school, led the youth group and retreats, witnessed mission work both near and far, and all who have been welcoming, inviting, and encouraging along the way. I can recall a lot of names, but most names and some faces have faded away.

How I Talk: Learning the Language

Among so many other things, our voices are literally shaped by those around us. I've lived where people say "y'all," and I end up saying it myself. I've lived where people say "yinz," and I say that, too. As a teen, I joined the throngs of adolescents who peppered their sentences with cool, rad, and a lot of other words I cannot type here. Beyond these silly vocabulary quirks, our voices in terms of what we have to say, and the way we say it, are impacted and influenced by others. The trick, for me at least, is finding the authentic voice that is inside all of us. It's easier said than done.

In terms of real and serious influence, one person who has left a deep and indelible imprint on my life, ministry, and voice is my dad. I am a "PK." Preacher's kids have all sorts of experiences and reputations. Some are choirboys and some are rebels. I'm not sure where I was in those regards, but what I am certain of is my dad's influence on my life of faith and my vocation as a pastor.

I would actually say the way he lives outside of work, if there is such a place for ministers, continues to impact me and, I hope, set an example for how to relate to others. That is by simply being a normal and relatable person that is fully human and with no pretentions about being fully divine. I recently saw the father of a childhood friend who said, "Andy, do you know what I remember liking most about your dad? It was that he was just a normal guy."

But it was, and still is, his voice in the pulpit, in the office, and around the Session table that stays with and continually influences me vocationally. I think it is normal that we either consciously or subconsciously emulate those we respect and just so happen to see and hear on a frequent (in my case with Dad, daily) basis. I soaked up his style, his creativity, and his sincerity in the pulpit that would at times challenge, but always remind the congregation that they are loved by God. Not a bad blueprint.

But here's the thing—Dad's the senior pastor at a church with well over two thousand members. Sitting in the pews growing up, that was hard not to notice. For a son who looks up to his dad, it is also hard not to be proud. Plus, he's been ordained since 1973, which is a long time. So while I do feel these are all very good, the reality is that it has taken me almost ten years of ministry to learn an important truth—I am not my dad. Nor should I expect to be.

Looking back to my seminary days, during my work at those field education churches, into my first call, and (truth be told) a lot of my second one as well, I can see that if I am brutally honest, I was subconsciously trying to be my dad. There probably is a list a mile long of psychologists who have earned their doctorate by studying this type of thing, and I'm sure there are obvious reasons why this may have happened to me. But, in a lot of ways, I can see how foolish I was to think that as I was just starting out I would be able to preach, teach, lead, care, and be a pastor like someone with close to forty years of ordained experience.

As I started in ministry, I infused my sermons with smart sounding Greek and Hebrew words to appear more intelligent. I quoted authors and preachers and even on occasion leaned heavily on one of Dad's old sermons to give off the illusion that I was actually that well read or that good of a preacher. The truth is much of the time I didn't really feel I knew what I was doing or talking about in sermons—not only in sermons but also in everything else. I remember one sermon at my field education church during my second year of seminary in which I referenced the "scrolls at Qumran" without the foggiest notion of anything having to do with the Dead Sea Scrolls.

The reality is I still do those things—use Greek and Hebrew, quote others, and have sermons influenced by some of Dad's thoughts. But instead of doing so to have a false authority or a borrowed voice, I am glad to be at a place in ministry that is authentically me with my own voice. That's not to say I'm still not influenced by Dad, and others, but it is to say that finally I am comfortable in my own robe. I mean vocational skin. How did this happen?

Perhaps a lot of it has to do with the confidence that comes with experience. The more I would do something, the more comfortable it became, and as a result, the more confident I would become in it. It's a simple formula. *Do something a lot, and it'll become a part of you.* This is nothing unusual as experience is the great teacher, and as it becomes a part of your identity, confidence is a characteristic of it. But I also think a lot of it has to do with feeling less and less like I have to "prove" myself and more and more like I can "be" myself. This feeling of having to prove myself was certainly not limited to my "father issues," as Mihee calls it. It extended to my seminary classmates as well. Sure, I was very comfortable in the dorm, playing intramurals in the gym and on the field, in the cafeteria, and around town. But when the opportunity for seniors came to preach in chapel, I gladly passed because I did not think I was good enough, funny enough, theologically sound enough, exegetically accurate enough, experienced enough, or confident enough to climb the five or six steps into that pulpit. This is something I have come to very much regret. It would have been an honor to proclaim God's word in that beautiful pulpit where many outstanding sermons have been preached by very gifted men and women. I miss not being able to say I lent my voice to that cloud of witnesses.

As I reflect on this more, I realize that I have been dealing with the feeling of needing to prove myself on and off again almost my whole life. Another reality of being a preacher's kid, and now a clergyman myself, is that I have moved around—a lot. Indiana is the eighth state I've called home, and that is including Pennsylvania, where I've lived twice. With each new start in a new location, as the new kid, new student, new guy, new pastor, and the like, finding my own place, footing, and voice was an initial barrier.

How I Live: Preaching and Practicing What I Preach

Traveling beside me in all of this for over a decade now has been Mihee. I have certainly been influenced by her unique and particular voice as well.

Her voice reminds me of a line in the old hymn "Wade in the Water" that speaks to God's "troubling" the water. As I think more about it, I have come to imagine this is a reference to God's active participation in this world. The still, peaceful, and easy waters of this world often invite us to a state of placidness. At the worst, we simply go along with the flow, afraid to deal with all of the challenges that come with making ripples, let alone waves. Perhaps God troubling the water causes us, or calls us, to the radical work that compels ordinary folks to drop their proverbial nets and follow a certain rabbi.

Mihee's prophetic voice has troubled the waters of what, I am sure, could have been, and at times still might be, a glassy-lake life and ministry. As we took classes like "Cultural Hermeneutics" together, and other classes in theology, she challenged me in a way that Calvin, Barth, or Augustine could not. I was suddenly engaged in and found myself thinking about, and talking about, issues that as a white middle-class suburban American male I had not had to wrestle with before. I looked at church, my preaching, my use of words, my relations with others, and the larger world in a way that was new to me.

I began to think about the power and the impact of one's voice. As she began serving her churches as an associate pastor, I really began to think about even the little comments we make to each other. This is because she would share with me some of what others have said to her—comments literally about her voice ("Talk louder and use the mic!"), or well-intentioned but condescending remarks about how young and cute she looked in her big black robe while leading worship ("just like my granddaughter!"). After we had been married for a few years, she was asked the question that is no one's business: "When are you going to have kids?" I've had my fair share of stupid comments about my beard or haircut or tie, but I can let those roll off after a few minutes of shaking my head. But when it happens to Mihee, something within me stirs to make sure that I am never that insensitive to another. I'm not sure I'd be aware of these things, or give them much thought, if I were not married to a member of the clergy.

Mihee's voice troubled the waters and, as a result, reshaped my ever-developing voice. I'm not going to lie and say it was, or is, an easy process. I saw things in myself and I listened to things about her life that are hard. But as these conversations, fights, and experiences played out, I have come to see that she has influenced me in ways that my dad, or anyone else for that matter, could not.

She has taught me that my voice is useless—a clanging gong or a noisy cymbal—if I don't back it up with action. If I don't "practice what I preach," as they say, then what good does it do? She has challenged me to be more courageous. She has challenged me to live with conviction. *She has challenged me to remain faithful (or at least try to) in the midst of hardship and the confusion that comes with asking "How long O Lord?"* Ultimately, she has shaped my voice just as much as, if not more than, my dad. I believe that this is due to the reality that she has gently pulled, pushed, and kicked me out of my zone of comfort and familiarity.

But, as I continue to grow in life, the more I can see that while I am influenced by, and who I am because of, many people, I am still God's unique creation—with my own voice.

I don't think there was a watershed moment for me when my voice became my own and I felt that I had clout. It has been a process that I am sure is still taking place. However, I do remember certain occasions in my first calls when I thought to myself, "Hold on a minute here. These people are actually taking me seriously and listening to what I have to say!" It was at the same time both frightening and exhilarating. Not that I am like them, but I wonder if young Timothy ever felt that way upon receiving Paul's letters and going forward in his ministry. I wonder if David, fresh from the fields with his ruddy complexion, ever felt that way as he was about to embark on the wild ride that was his ministry. Actually, as he was transfigured on the mountain, I wonder how Jesus felt as he had his authority confirmed when the voice from heaven said, "Listen to him." As a member of the clergy, knowing that people listen to and follow your voice is a humbling proposition.

Someone with more wisdom than me once reminded me of something as I had just came to the end of what we Presbyterians refer to as "the call process." They said, "Andy, this church has called you. They interviewed you. They spent time with you. They listened to you. They like you. They called you—and no one else. Claim and live into that reality." Those words echo in my mind with frequency as I seek to live out my ministry with my own authority and my own unique voice. And that person was right. God has equipped me with my own thoughts, feelings, emotions, and, yes, voice. Claiming that has been freeing as well as empowering.

If the Bible is right in saying that we are shapeable clay, then I'm glad that God is the kind of potter who shapes my voice by placing people close to me who can influence it. I pray for the wisdom to discern who to listen to and soak in, and who to forget. And, whatever clout my voice may carry, however it sounds, and whatever it may be, my urgent prayer is simply this: "May the words of my mouth . . . be pleasing and acceptable to you, O Lord, our rock and redeemer." *Amen.*

MIHEE KIM-KORT

> Before I can tell my life what I want to do with it, I must listen to my
> life telling me who I am.
>
> —Parker J. Palmer[2]

A baby's baptism.

It was the first time I saw Andy lead worship as an ordained minister. He was not preaching that morning, and I needed to eventually get to my job (I was working part-time as a barista at a Starbucks near the high school), so I stayed for the beginning of the service. I knew he was scheduled to do a baptism for the first time, and I felt the need to be a part of that milestone. I also wanted to see him in that official capacity, administering what I call one of the "job perks" of ordained ministry. Baptism seemed to be one of those untouchable rites that in my pre-seminary mind meant that clergy had some kind of special power, and that the whole ritual called on something supernatural and magical. I realize now that baptisms are pretty ordinary, but they do have their own magic in how they provide a glimpse into eternity—and it was special and a privilege for clergy to be a part of it.

On this particular morning, I remember being struck by his presence, and his ease in front of the congregation. His joy radiating from every cell in his body. His capable hands pouring out the water dramatically. His intentional pouring of the water, and the sound of it splashing into the font was compelling; every word and act was clearly deliberate and thoughtful. His hands surprisingly confident while holding what seemed like the tiniest baby (and this was way before we had our own). His proclamation that this little creature was a child of God graciously punctuated with a gentle kiss on the forehead. The quiet "aw" and "oh" response from the congregation that perfectly matched the sweetness of the experience. It could not have gone more smoothly, and no doubt, this treasured moment would remain indelibly imprinted on the minds of the baby's parents.

I watched, wondering what it would be like for me up there someday.

I was despairing a little at the time. Graduation from seminary seemed years ago, and as I continued to interview at various churches in the area for any and all positions, I had mixed feelings watching Andy. On the one hand, I couldn't be more excited for him—he was obviously created for this vocation, but still worked incredibly hard and approached everything with a new seriousness and maturity. The community welcomed him and supported his ministry, as well as giving him space to make mistakes (not that he made many) and ask questions (as a thoughtful person he asked many). Few things were more gratifying than seeing him thrive and flourish in this place. On the other hand, I felt acutely that I had worked just as hard, if not harder in some instances because of the inevitable double standard. And I was still waiting on the proverbial sidelines, gear on and my shoes laced up, hoping for a chance to get out on the field. I was ready. I gushed and listened and conveyed my passion at each interview. But apparently no church was ready for me.

Both of us eventually received first calls to churches to become associate pastors. Much later, after Andy received his call and began work at Larchmont, I finally took a call at a church in New Jersey, which meant more than a two-hour round-trip commute. While Andy's position was a generalist position, there was an expectation that his focus would be on youth. My call was specifically for youth and Christian education, even though there were a whole host of other responsibilities. This significant beginning was where we overlapped, but it was the only place.

As I catapulted myself into ministry, I found every aspect exhilarating: Sunday worship services, gatherings with youth, even—gasp!—Session meetings. But I was terribly uncertain. When should I speak up in Bible studies? How much can I try to change in the current youth group? What am I supposed to say before everyone needs to sit down after the passing of the peace?

Learning the Right Volume: My Voice

Listening to others was a skill that I acquired early on. It was impressed on me as an important life skill. Listening to my teachers. Listening to my parents. Listening to my pastors. Listening to everyone but myself.

However, discovering my voice and learning to *embrace* it was not an easy process. Although Andy had grown up in a church where all the pastoral staff were women besides his father, I had only recently seen a woman preach in the pulpit as an ordained minister for the first time. It blew his mind that I had not heard a woman preach before, while he wouldn't even bat an eye at it. I floundered quite a bit in the speech and homiletics courses in seminary as I tried on different voices, like so many pairs of shoes. I don't think anyone noticed, but Andy often said that he thought I had two voices. One was my "cute" voice, and the other was my "*jundo*" (the shortened Korean word for student pastor) voice. Apparently, I used my cute voice a lot with him, and it seemed pretty effective in terms of getting him to do what I wanted at the time. My *jundo* voice was a few octaves lower, and it was my serious, mature voice. I didn't realize I had these two voices for different contexts and wondered if I needed to find a way to unify them and be a consistent presence. How would I learn to do this honestly and effectively?

Once again, I was hard pressed to find a role model that truly fit since my instructors were all white, male, and much older. No one had a voice that I could imitate in a way that would seem consistent with who I am. But I continued to experiment, not only in preaching classes but in all my classes, by pushing myself to speak up during discussions no matter how reluctant I felt at the time.

When I began at my first call at the medium-sized church in New Jersey, I found I was constantly self-conscious about how I sounded to the congregation. I was nervous. Awkward, mostly. And squeaky. It didn't help when many of the older congregation members tried to encourage me by saying things like:

"We're just so used to [the head pastor] and his voice."
"Just speak more slowly."
"It might help to lower your voice."
"I know you can do it. Just speak up more."

This caused me to struggle with major cotton-mouth before each worship service. I tried to overcompensate by changing my voice to be either higher or lower. And while it did get easier to be in the pulpit, and I felt less nervous each week, I still didn't *feel myself*.

Even though I continued to hear the same sentiments from these older members, I also began to hear positive comments like "Your voice is so soothing" and "You have a nice speaking voice." But instead of being helpful, this confused me. I was at a loss. They didn't seem like compliments—if anything, they almost seemed like sympathy, as if they were telling me that my voice was still a distraction to my sermons. Should I speak at a higher register? Should I add more breathiness? Should I modulate my voice? Should I speak slowly and annunciate each syllable? More often than not, I just couldn't tell which voice was more me. Either way, my presence in the pulpit felt forced and affected, and I hated that feeling. I wanted to be confident and self-assured, authentic and transparent, and not have to squeeze myself into someone else's fancy high heels.

Andy and I talked often about this issue. It didn't seem as much of a concern for him, personally, but he could see that I wrestled with it on a regular basis. He would give me pointers, but talking in front of people came so naturally to him. Even though he had most of his worship parts scripted out and neatly kept in a black professional binder, he didn't seem to rely on it. I mimicked him, highlighting my parts in the bulletin, printing out a script, and keeping it in a nondescript binder of my own. It was an anchor in some ways, but also a crutch. Though it was something for me to depend on, it felt more like an artificial appendage. I grew frustrated. I realized that in my effort to not rely on my head pastor's example, or any other colleague or instructor in worship, I was inadvertently imitating Andy and his demeanor, his posture, and his energy in worship. It was the closest, safest solution for me, and it seemed like the best pair of shoes to slip on, even though I knew it wasn't a good fit. I finally acknowledged I knew I needed something else to carry me on this journey.

Living into the Authority: My Vocation

I am Me. In all the world, there is no one else exactly like me. Everything that comes out of me is authentically mine, because I alone chose it—I own everything about me: my body, my feelings, my mouth, my voice, all my actions, whether they be to others or myself. I own my fantasies, my dreams, my hopes, my fears. I own my triumphs and successes, all my failures and mistakes. Because I own all of me, I can become intimately acquainted with me . . . I own me, and therefore, I can engineer me. I am me, and I am okay.

—Virginia Satir[3]

The first time I felt like a pastor was at a high school youth retreat many years later. By then I was at my second call and had been with this group of kids for some years. We were outside standing in line for a "ride" called the Screamer, a huge swing that allowed for the sensation of a brief free-fall. It was jam-packed and cold, and incredibly loud, as though the youth were trying to keep themselves warm by yelling and shouting jokes at each other. For a moment I turned to talk to some of our own in the back of the line. And I heard, "Pastor! Pastor!"

It was an older woman's voice, probably one of the program staff or maybe an advisor. I didn't totally recognize it. Still, I instinctively turned back around. When I looked up and saw it was a leader from another church, I turned away. I paused and quickly processed how I responded to that label. I had never done that before. It felt good. It felt right. And because I didn't dwell on it too much, it felt normal. Before, anytime I'd heard someone calling for the pastor, I looked around trying to find who else could be a pastor. Whenever I was in the office while the other pastor was out, and someone came in looking for a pastor, I would automatically say, "He's out for the day at meetings." It took some time to say, instead, "I'm a pastor at this church, too. Can I help you with something?" It took even longer to brush off the surprised look on the visitor's face, and struggle through those first moments of awkward responses:

"Oh, well, I'll leave a message with you for the other pastor."
"Oh, um, well, are you the youth pastor?"
"Oh, I need help with something that only he can give me."

This process was long and painful. But to finally get to the point at which I saw myself as a pastor, and have it actually integrated into my identity, was gratifying and exciting, and even more so when I discovered I could simply be fully *myself*. Not my father. Not my husband. Not even other older woman pastors in the presbytery. God's call to me to this vocation and letting myself wear it, not just as a fancy new accessory or vestment but also as something that permeated my entire identity—it was my desire for myself. Confidence and authority didn't mean exuding ego or pride, having a certain arrogant vibe, or even cultivating a loud voice.

It meant being totally and fully me. The best model ended up being Christ Incarnate: Jesus being fully human and fully divine suddenly meant being fully himself. And this called out to me.

Eventually, I found intentional ways to cultivate my authority through cultivating my voice. They went hand in hand. And it meant more than the volume—it also meant the connection and content. *This became the priority in my journey not only in the pulpit but also every time I would speak up—feeling connected to what I was saying, and not worrying about the tone or level.* I found that when I truly felt what I was saying deep in my bones that whatever authority I sought to convey in my life was already present. I didn't have to find a source outside, but just needed to be open to that voice inside me. I didn't need to rely on anyone's authority, or to bend or try to fit myself into someone else's mold.

More importantly, I discovered in not needing to fill someone else's huge shoes, in learning about my own voice, I needed to learn to *listen*, first and foremost. I listened to God's spirit in me. I listened to my own heart and passions. I listened to the stories of those like me who were struggling to find their own voices and authority. And I could finally comfortably listen to and *receive* Andy's affirmation and feel the truth in his words for me. He helped me to be open to my own story and the way it would shape my voice in a unique way. He provided a space for me to articulate that story. And he urged me in his own way to seek out that one necessity in life that would make me succumb to that Something truly greater than me—one who would not burden me with the world's standards, but make me who I am. Make me, not only as a pastor but also as a woman, a mother, a daughter, and a human being.

AFTERWORDS

> I think it would be well, and proper, and obedient, and pure, to grasp your one necessity and not let it go, to dangle from it limp wherever it takes you.
>
> —Annie Dillard[4]

By nature seminarians (and pastors) read a lot of books written by a lot of different authors. They listen to lectures by many professors. They are surrounded by others in their classes, study groups, the cafeteria, and in the dorms. They listen to countless sermons by different preachers, and probably have one or two favorites. Likely they entered seminary because they were influenced by a pastor back home in their own church. The number of "voices" a seminarian, or even pastor, encounters is significant. Clearly some have more sway than others.

While we have found our own voices, we are still influenced by one another, and work hard to make sure it is in a good and constructive way. Mihee reads and listens to my sermons and gives helpful feedback and constructive advice. Likewise, I will read and give feedback on Mihee's blogs, writings, and sermons. It's not limited to the ways we use our voices in formal settings. We process potential conversations with co-workers or congregants. We craft language for moderating meetings. We practice possible ways to encourage those around us. As ministers of the Word and Sacrament, we try to remind each other how sacred and important our voices are to God's kingdom, and make space to cultivate it within our relationship.

—AK

CONNECT

- Who has influenced your "voice" the most in life and in ministry? Why do you think they have had such a profound effect on you?
- Do you see yourself overlapping with their style? Is that a positive or a negative in your mind? How can, or have, you differentiate(d) yourself from those people and voices that influence you?
- In the Great Commission, Jesus declares, "All authority in heaven and on earth has been given to me." Do you think authority is given to you or do you have to earn it?
- Do you struggle with authority or does it come naturally? Being careful not to be a "know-it-all," how do you share what you know while at the same time being open to the reality that others have much to share as well?

3

CHARISMA

Making Space for Each Ministry Style

MIHEE KIM-KORT

> You were born together, and together you shall be forevermore. You shall be together when the white wings of death scatter your days. Ay, you shall be together even in the silent memory of God. But let there be spaces in your togetherness, And let the winds of the heavens dance between you.

—Khalil Gibran, "On Marriage"[1]

Few people have described me as charismatic.

And I have personally never used that to characterize myself. In my mind, it was a word for preachers and evangelists that drew multitudes into auditoriums and gyms. For musicians who would walk on stage and cause people to swoon and pass out. For celebrities, actors, politicians, all those naturally inclined to be in front of others and *be so attractive to everyone,* male and female, young and old. For teachers and motivational speakers that made their audiences laugh and cry and walk out of the room with a renewed sense of purpose. I don't mind public speaking, but I have never really had that *energy* or *enthusiasm* that was contagious and made the room light up.

In secular use, the word is not terribly useful. It has a Pied Piper superficiality to it. In theological terms, it has some potential traction when it comes to understanding who we are as individuals in this particular calling. As I understand it in our Reformed tradition, charisma has roots in the Greek word *charisma*, which means "a divinely given gift, power, or ability." While it may be a more visible part of other traditions, it does fit within a Reformed sense of providence. All gifts are from God. Although we may be a bit skittish about a wild pneumatology, we have an expansive view of charisma since it is possible and available to the priesthood of all believers.

Andy and I obviously have different charismas. There was no doubt about that fact from the beginning. I have often joked that he is the public face of the "company" and I'm the brains. But this kind of pigeon-holing isn't completely accurate, as our roles are often fluid and our styles and personalities allow for blurred lines. Still, it requires a posture of graciousness toward each other, and by graciousness, I mostly mean like the grace of a dancer—flexibility. So it is no coincidence that charisma also has roots in the Greek word *charis*, which means, "grace." What this often meant for us was realizing how indispensable grace would be in our marriage and ministry. It was and is grace that allows us to make space for one another to live into our own specific gifts and ministries.

Discovering Charisma: Coming Alive

The moments I felt the most alive had little to do with adrenaline or spotlights. They mostly had to do with being with people in quiet moments, whether in prayer or on a walk, in the dim light of a cabin full of adolescent girls asking questions about God and grace at the end of a retreat, in the remote wilderness of the San Juan mountains with a small group bundled up in sleeping bags around a campfire and under a sky full of shooting stars. In college, I felt a bit of that light and fire, but couldn't quite pinpoint what it was that made me so excited.

When I finally went away to seminary and met Andy, I came face-to-face with someone so impossibly different, who grew up in such a different context and lifestyle and community, that I wondered: Would we find anything in common? And why was I so attracted to him? Was the old adage "opposites attract" really true? Not only did we come from very different ethnic and geographic cultures, but he was also twenty-seven when I first met him. He had graduated from college the year I graduated from high school. He had worked for a number of years before going to seminary, while I had gone a year after graduation. He grew up in a mainline experience of the church, while I grew up in a Korean church. He listened to old school rap and the Cure, while I loved the Indigo Girls and what I now call "Jesus music" (contemporary praise and worship music). But we were so different that it actually compelled us to see and articulate our lives in new ways. He would ask me questions I had never considered before. So it was in our relationship I discovered the space to practice verbalizing what exactly made me come alive, but also what was coming alive in me.

During the summers between the academic year, Andy and I did internships to fulfill both school and ordination requirements. I went away to my beloved Colorado to work as a backpacking guide for Wilderness Ranch, a Young Life camp that ministers to high school students during seven-day excursions. Andy went to work at a small, diverse, urban church in South Boston. While I was leading a group of high school students and adults up a mountain that was over 13,500 feet in elevation, Andy was leading and trying to keep together a group of thirty preschool-aged children through the maze that was the "T" (the subway system in Boston) to get to the aquarium. While I was setting up climbs for students to rock climb and rappel—most for the first time in their lives—up and down a huge boulder, Andy was leading songs and chants during the Summer Meals Program closing assembly for hundreds of neighborhood children. While I was waking up at 5 a.m. before the sunrise to get water and begin boiling it for breakfast, Andy was rolling out of a hideaway couch bed in the church's minister's home and getting ready for another full day of songs, art, play, and serving meals to many children whose only meal that day would be the one they got from the church.

I remember getting mail from him during my first summer in Creed, Colorado, which was the little town closest to base camp for the ranch. Andy and I wrote letters to each other, sent postcards, and so forth. For fun, we each took pictures of our lives in our ministries and communities with disposable cameras, and sent them to each other to develop in our respective places. When I picked up his pictures at the little store in Creed, I felt something tugging at my heart. It was a few things. I was a little envious of his experience in the urban setting. I tried to imagine what it would be like to be there in his shoes. But most of all, I was so thrilled to see him thriving in ministry. I loved the photos of him on the subway or playing with kids of all colors or with the minister's family. He looked so alive.

Later when we were able to talk on the phone, it was funny the way he shared the same sentiments. He talked about the mountains surrounding our cabins, and the joy and light that I was radiating surrounded by guides and high school students. There was something so special about sharing these seasons together, and the affirmation we offered each other deepened those unique experiences. Our contexts were completely different, and yet there was so much to reflect on together. I felt an intense interest in what Andy was doing in this multi-cultural church, and Andy offered his own reflections on different possibilities for engaging the experience theologically. But it was the stories we shared with each other—and the space we made for these stories—that helped us to realize what it was about those communities that stirred a distinct kind of light and life in us. It was the conversations—the words, the questions, the responses, the answers, the pauses and quiet—almost a physical shaping and molding of space that allowed for moments of revelation, and ones that I believe I would never have had with another person in the same way. I'm certain that I wouldn't have had the same experience of discovering that fire without the space Andy created for me.

Making Space for Each Other's Charisma: Occupy Grace

"Occupy Wall Street."

I remember those signs. Photos of people holding up those signs on Wall Street, and then all around the country, clogged up my newsfeed. I picked up the following description from the all-knowing Wikipedia:

> The Canadian activist group Adbusters initiated the protest, which subsequently led to Occupy protests and movements around the world. The main issues are social and economic inequality, greed, corruption and the perceived undue influence of corporations on government— particularly from the financial services sector. The OWS slogan, We are the 99%, addresses the growing income inequality and wealth distribution in the U.S. between the wealthiest 1% and the rest of the population. To achieve their goals, protesters act on consensus-based decisions made in general assemblies which emphasize direct action over petitioning authorities for redress. [2]

Something about these movements spoke to me. I wanted to be there with people who were passionate—mad—about a certain cause. I longed to feel the energy of such a gathering. I imagined that few things would be more inspiring. It made me remember the last time these kind of demonstrations happened nearby. I was in seminary when the United States invaded Iraq in 2003. There constantly were posters and emails about the location and details of the next protest—in Philadelphia, in New York City, right in downtown Princeton. Afterward, stories about who was there—students and faculty—what happened, and who almost got arrested, circulated the community.

I never went to one.

I should have gone. I wanted to be a part of it. I wanted to tell a couple of friends who invited me, to those people in Iraq whose lives and communities would be changed forever: "I'm there with you." But the thought of being in that space was overwhelming. So I stayed back. I regret it. When these Occupy movements began to pop up around the country, I felt the same anxiety. I tried to show support by *tweeting* and *re-tweeting* information about it all as much as possible, and *liking* various posts on Facebook. Social media makes a huge difference when it comes to connecting with certain happenings, but of course, it didn't feel quite the same as it probably would have if I had bodily been there. Still, I bring it up here because of what it makes me think of in relationship to marriage and ministry, calling and family.

It has a little bit to do with all the debates about connection—social media versus face-to-face. I am certain that the majority of people in this world wouldn't hesitate to agree that face-to-face is the best way to connect with someone. But there is something to be said about the particularly distinct feeling of community that people experience "virtually." Perhaps the issue is balance, and realizing that the world we live in now almost obligates us to do and use both. To occupy both spaces. My father recently got an iPhone, and now we text each other daily. That mode of communication—and connection—doesn't replace phone calls or Skype or, God forbid, actual visits, but in many ways, it enhances them.

All this is to say that even though the various modes of connection have become incredibly diverse within a marriage and partnership, it isn't enough to simply text or email to "check in." Andy and I sometimes find ourselves falling into that habit when the weeks are busy, and while that at least affords us some chance to touch base, we've realized time and time again that it isn't enough. And when we don't hear each other's voices or see each other's faces, and when we're not able to give a reassuring hug or squeeze of the hand, we turn into roommates who are living together and sharing responsibilities for the care of our family and home in a way that is absent of grace.

So the Occupy movement speaks to me of incarnation—the power of physicality and bodies, and the impact of flesh and blood and breath. Likewise, I can't imagine or understand grace without incarnation. To occupy grace in the context of our life together means to intentionally and bodily carve out a space for my partner to discover and live into his charisma. No agendas on my part. No plans on my part. No expectations or standards on my part. It means that sometimes I have to step out of the way. It means sometimes I have to say, "You need to do to that interview and seek out what is there," when I am uncertain about my own call and what it would mean if we followed that road to his new call. It means sometimes I have to trust that occupying grace means embracing new possibilities, new paths, new ways of being and doing as a couple, as ministers, and, most importantly and recently, as parents. It sometimes means throwing caution to the wind and embracing the madness of grace, and what it means to be incarnationally joined to another. Indeed, extending that grace first and foremost to Andy says, "I'm there with you." And sometimes that is all one needs from your partner.

ANDY KORT

> The only people for me are the mad ones, the ones who are mad to live, mad to talk, mad to be saved, desirous of everything at the same time, the ones who never yawn or say a commonplace thing, but burn, burn, burn, like fabulous yellow roman candles exploding like spiders across the stars and in the middle you see the blue centerlight pop and everybody goes "Awww!"
>
> —Jack Kerouac[3]

In my premarital counseling sessions with couples, we discuss the importance of remembering that, although we become (or, in our case, are) married, two do not necessarily become one. Every relationship consists of two individuals. These individuals were raised in different families, often in different cities and parts of the country. They most likely have different likes and dislikes. In my sessions with these soon to be married couples, I always ask them, among other questions, to verbalize something they both enjoy doing together. They'll rattle off activities, such as watching movies, exercising, camping, or skiing. I follow that question by asking them to name an activity they relish doing that their partner does not. One likes wine, the other likes beer. One likes walks on the beach, the other likes surfing. One likes art museums, the other likes cafes. One likes shopping, the other likes fishing.

The hope is to help them understand that although they will soon share a mailing address (if they don't already), they do, and will, have some different likes and preferences than their partner. On the rare occasion I have a couple tell me that they enjoy everything the other does and they like doing every single thing together, I try not to roll my eyes as I think to myself, "Whether you know it or not, you are lying." And then I push them to keep thinking. Eventually, they will come up with something. Finally, we converse about the need to create space to allow their partner to engage in those life giving activities. In many ways, it has to do with giving your partner the freedom and flexibility to be who they are without trying to manipulate them into the way you think they should be, or worse, to be like you.

When Mihee and I did our premarital counseling sessions with the minister—who also happened to be the dean of student life and community at the seminary, and eventually a good friend—she simply asked us questions. And they were questions we had not considered together—for instance, what we thought about finances, and how to manage them. Or how we deal with anger and conflict—that is, what would our fighting be like? Because marriage was more than about understanding each other's likes and dislikes, it also had to do with knowing each other's habits and inclinations, strengths and weaknesses. I remember a story she would tell us often, and that we often share with others who are engaged to be married. It was about how she and her husband put the toothpaste cap on. She absolutely hated the way her husband put the toothpaste cap on, and even jokingly felt pretty murderous about it. This made us laugh. Now we have our own stories to share about those little idiosyncrasies. Few things drive me more insane than the way Mihee puts on a new roll of toilet paper or hangs up towels or doesn't have a consistent place to put her keys. But I am also fully aware that I am somewhat anal about many things. I drink directly from the huge bottles of juice in the fridge. I always call her for directions anywhere—to her constant chagrin.

But this is part of love, isn't it?

Making Space: Opposite Attraction

In many ways whoever coined the phrase "opposites attract" had it right. If there was a Wikipedia page for it, our names would certainly be on the list of examples. For Mihee and me, this is without question true when it comes to our ministry styles. It is challenging for me to think of another area in our life together where we are more different. To be clear, we are different in many areas—not only ministry but also our hobbies and our interests—of our life together. We find out and realize more and more just how different we are the longer we are together. But we've always been okay with it. I don't think we are necessarily called to marry, let alone minister, with people who are exactly like us in every way.

Backing up a little, I do think we have to acknowledge there is much that overlaps in our ministries, lives, and even personalities. I'm not totally from Mars, and she's not totally from Venus. Obviously, we do have much cohesion in our life together. These are some of the things that initially attracted me to Mihee. Going beyond our everyday likes and dislikes, the deeper you travel into our hearts the more you can see what we do have in common. We are on the same page in terms of politics, theology, hopes and dreams for our children and family. We desire the same thing for our ministries. The rub comes in the way we are inclined to get there and to live into these realities, hopes, and dreams.

And, my goodness, is there ever a rub. Of course, what happens when there is a rub? Friction. The more rubbing and friction there is, the more heat is produced in the midst of those two objects. I'm told this is basic physics. We've had our fair share of friction, conflict, and conflicting approaches as we engage ministry together. Early on, it was common, and sometimes still is, for frustration with the other to enter the picture. Common questions included "Why won't you just do it my way?" or "Why are you doing it like that?" The root of the frustration is found not in the other person, but rather, the other's reluctance to do it the way we would do it.

Clearly, this is not limited to clergy couples. Working with other staff we see that we often engage ministry in different ways and the need for balance between styles is crucial. If you have spent much time in a local congregation, you will likely see the different ministry styles among the members and the clergy. The one main difference is that I don't have to go home and eat dinner with members of the congregation or my colleagues from work night in and night out.

Even Jesus had to navigate the rub of various ministry styles. In Mark's ninth chapter, John rushes up to Jesus and says, "Teacher, we saw someone casting out demons in your name, and we tried to stop him, because he was not following us."[4] In my mind's eye, I can see John saying something along the lines of, "Jesus! We saw someone doing ministry, and we tried to stop him, because he wasn't one of us and he wasn't doing it like we do! Jesus, don't you think you should tell him to cut it out and do it like we do?" I imagine Jesus once again chuckling as the disciples just don't get it. He tells John, "Do not stop him . . . whoever is not against us is for us."[5]

Jesus allows space for those who "do ministry" even though they aren't "one of us." This speaks to me when I think of interdenominational relations. This very much challenges me when I think of those who "do ministry, and not like we do it." Jesus's words cut deep and touch a nerve especially when thinking about those I disagree with, how they do ministry in Jesus's name, and what they teach. At a deeper level, I have fundamental issues with those who do not value women in leadership, who scare people into believing in Jesus with "turn or burn theology," who claim to have every single answer and those who demonize others who are not like them. Sometimes, we are like John. We are convinced we are the one who is with Jesus and doing ministry as it should be done. Other times we are like the man accused of doing ministry while "not being one of us."

Making Space: Different Styles

With Mihee and me, it is not a matter of differing beliefs as much as it is a matter of differing styles. I don't know how I would describe her style. It is hard to pin down. She's at the same time a perfectionist and scattered all over the place. She is laissez-faire while liking to have a pile of details in place. She is laid back and always with an overflowing plate of commitments and obligations. It drives me crazy. And while she can tell you I have spoken out against her ways, I can tell you my tongue has scars from biting it so often. But, because I have witnessed her minister in great ways, I find that I am biting my tongue and getting frustrated with her less and less often as we get deeper into our respective ministries.

I think this is due to a realization that all those who seek to minister in Jesus's name come to know and understand. Ministry is hard. Being a member of the clergy can be the best job in the world, rate highly on job satisfaction surveys, and give joys that I am certain are only embraced and understood by those with this calling. But let me say it again: Ministry is hard. It can be draining physically, emotionally, and spiritually. It can be frustrating beyond belief and make one wonder why they ever went to seminary in the first place. Is it too late for law school? Ministry calls us to make sacrifices, and often family and friends are the casualties. It is hard to be unable to attend functions and reunions with friends out of town or extended family because Easter and Christmas are heavy work times. We can't easily travel then. Oh, and did I mention that we work weekends, too? Sorry not to be able to make that cookout or go to the party. Count yourself lucky if you have family and friends who understand the unique challenges for clergy. But I am not complaining. I love this calling.

What I do dislike however is how hard some in our congregations make ministry. I have seen and heard stories about how clergy are horribly mistreated. Thankfully, most have stayed in the ministry, but many have left—and not just young pastors. Discussions in the parking lot, secret meetings in homes, struggles for power, and other things that happen behind our backs can cause one's guard to go up. We also get it to our faces—cutting comments while shaking hands at the end of the service or in the fellowship hall during coffee hour often come with a smile. Anonymous notes, letters, and voicemail messages likewise come our way with well-thought-out criticisms, comments, and suggestions. I always wonder how the mystery mailers expect us to follow up with them without a return address, name, or phone number. (When this happens to me, I later realize that it is a blessing that I cannot follow up because I fear my temper would get the best of me and I would actually let them know what I think of them.) Others sabotage good plans and ideas because of a grudge or their own personal issue. Others will derail conversations. Still others push their agendas with an unrelenting force. Ministry is hard and sometimes those whom we are called to minister to don't make it any easier. I have been incredibly blessed to work at three relatively healthy and very supportive churches. I have been encouraged, allowed to make mistakes, and have been shown more grace than I deserve. Even in the best situations, ministry is not easy.

And that is a significant reason why I try not to make it any harder on Mihee. It's challenging enough without her own spouse giving her the business all the time. I know enough to put my know-it-all tendencies on the shelf. I have had to learn to let her have her space and to do ministry as she discerns it needs to be done, even if I would do it differently. I've also seen times when I have been wrong. Those occurrences now seem to happen with an alarming rate of frequency. It is humbling, yet also thrilling, to see her in these moments.

While in my opinion there are some very bad and dangerous ministry styles out there, what I have learned in ministry is that there is not one exact right or wrong way to do ministry. What works in one context might not work in another. One pastor may be wildly successful in one faith community and fall flat on his face while using the same style in another. Ultimately, the different styles are a something like a gift. Not a gift to us, but the children of God who encounter us in ministry. I know my style doesn't work well for everyone. Nor does Mihee's. However, as the Body of Christ gathers together, it is a cross-section of humanity. They not only seek but also need different styles and ways of ministry in order to see and understand more fully the grace of God. Mihee constantly challenges me to self-reflect and to see, sometimes for better or for worse, why I do what I do in ministry. I hope I do that for her.

The truth of the matter is I have seen her effortlessly connect with people in a way I cannot and vice versa. As I am sure you have determined by now, her writing is beautiful, clear, creative, and far better than mine. We have different gifts. We have similar gifts. And we work hard to complement one another, realizing that is not a given because of opposite personalities or gifts, but rather something that has to constantly be cultivated in every season.

Finally, I am reminded time and again that God has prepared Mihee in a different way than God has prepared me. Through her background, family history, experience with race and gender issues, the Potter has created and molded something far different—not better, not worse—than the often broken vessel that is me. And I can't deny that. And I can't pretend that there is not a need for her and her style of ministry, because there is a need as I have seen time and time again. So, once again, this is another case in which I'd be wise to listen to Jesus, even though Mihee does ministry in his name, but not like me. If I listen closely, I think I can hear him whisper in my ear, "Don't stop her." Who am I to stand in her way?

AFTERWORDS

We were not created to be automatons—all the same, functioning exactly the same way, with the same likes and the same talents. We were each created individually with our own gifts, skills, abilities, interests, and passions. Clearly, these oftentimes will overlap, which is great. However, as Paul describes in the familiar passage on the body in 1 Corinthians 12, there are varieties of gifts and there are varieties of activities. Unless serving as co-pastors who work together to fill one ministry position that fulfills one job description, clergy working together—married to each other or not—are usually not charged with doing the same thing. Likewise, at a multi-staff church one will do "this" while another does "that."

Yet, for some, it can be difficult to allow the space for another to flourish in their gifts. We get in their way. We become convinced that the way we do it is the best way. But odds are good that we think our way is the best way because that is the way we know best. And it may be a good way, one that has worked well previously. Or maybe we consider one, or more, particular area of ministry to be "our thing." We think to ourselves, "I should be the one involved in all of the mission work and leadership." In some cases, we run the risk of thinking of ourselves a little too highly while at the same time thinking a little lesser of others.

So perhaps it's a practice of humility. Sitting down, moving aside, and getting out of the way, to make room for someone else's gifts, talents, and abilities.

—AK

CONNECT

- How do you navigate and allow for complimentary gifts, skills, and so on to overlap?
- Where do you see friction in this process with your ministry partner?

- Is sacrificing an area of strength so that another can lead ministry in that same area hard for you? Why? Should we even sacrifice an area of strength in the first place?
- What are some things you do that allow you to recognize gifts and skills in someone else?
- Are pride and ego ever a stumbling block for you in ministry?
- Who has given you space and room for your style in your journey thus far?

4

CAUTION

Creating Realistic Boundaries with Church Members

ANDY KORT

There are two vivid scenes in one of my favorite movies, *Field of Dreams*, dealing with boundaries. The first takes place on the night that Shoeless Joe Jackson, played by Ray Liotta, shows up to play baseball on the field created by the farmer, Ray Kinsella (Kevin Costner). Earlier, Kinsella had plowed under his major crop (corn) to build this baseball field after hearing a voice telling him, "If you build it, he will come." In a leap of faith, he builds it. Finally, after months of waiting, Joe Jackson comes. As Jackson is poking around on the infield dirt and in the cool of the outfield grass, Kinsella rushes out to the field to meet and ultimately hit fly balls and pitch to Jackson. This is a dreamlike sequence on many levels, and it crosses the boundaries of both space and time, as well as reality and fantasy. You see, Joe Jackson died in 1951. Kinsella builds the field in Iowa in 1988. And yet there is Jackson running toward him after breaking through the boundary of the outfield corn and into Kinsella's life.

As the two throw and hit balls back and forth, eventually Kinsella's wife and daughter emerge from their farmhouse and come down to the field. They, too, can see the ghostlike Jackson. Ray introduces Shoeless Joe to his wife and daughter, who immediately invite him inside for something to drink. The camera flashes down to Jackson's black spikes that stand with his toes on the boundary of the dreamlike baseball field and reality of the rest of Kinsella's property. Jackson quickly glances down at his shoes and then backs up as he says, "I can't." If he is to continue living out his dream of playing baseball again, he is literally unable to cross the threshold of the boundary laid before him in limestone chalk and dirt. He can't leave the field.

The other scene takes place in the exact same location on the field. The boundary is the same and the consequence of crossing the boundary is the same. For the ballplayer, crossing that line of demarcation prevents them from ever returning and playing on this field of dreams again. They would be destined to life in reality as the rest of us know it. This time Kinsella's daughter, Karen, falls off the top of the bleachers while watching the game. She lands on her back and begins to choke on her hot dog. One of the players, Archie "Moonlight" Graham, is a young rookie on the diamond but had become a doctor in his later life. As Karen lies on the ground choking and her mother rushes off to call an ambulance, Graham approaches the boundary. He is faced with the same reality Shoeless Joe was earlier: If he stays behind the line, he can keep playing and living out his dream of playing ball with the major leaguers. If he crosses the line and breaks the boundary, his playing days are over.

The camera once again quickly pans down to his feet and then back up to Graham's knowing face. As the camera flashes back down to Graham's feet, we see him take a bold step to cross the boundary from the field of dreams to reality. His black spikes transform into black loafers, and his white cotton ball pants transform into neatly creased brown slacks. Instead of carrying his leather glove, Graham is suddenly carrying his leather doctor's bag. He walks over, sits Karen up, pounds her on the back, and discards the piece of hot dog that was lodged in her throat. As the emotion settles back down to a calm state, the realization falls on everyone—Graham can't go back. He is no longer "Moonlight Graham." He is "Doc Graham."

Crossing Boundaries: Dealing with Consequences

Life is complex. Each one of us must make his own path through life. There are no self-help manuals, no formulas, no easy answers. The right road for one is the wrong road for another. . . . The journey of life is not paved in blacktop; it is not brightly lit, and it has no road signs. It is a rocky path through the wilderness.

—M. Scott Peck[1]

While there is so much to mine here in terms of identity, dreams, and choices, I felt compelled by the image of those lines, and what they could mean for ministry and community. Namely, it is a way to think about how every relationship with a church member has these lines, and what they mean in both positive and negative ways.

As Shoeless Joe and Moonlight Graham show us, crossing boundaries has consequences. Every time we approach a boundary, we face a decision that impacts our lives and sometimes the lives of others. Shoeless Joe decided not to cross. Graham went forward and crossed. We could argue that Graham made the better, more loving, compassionate, self-sacrificing choice. His baseball life was now over, but his life as a doctor was enlivened (and Karen's life saved). We could argue that in this case, as well as in many others, boundaries should and must be broken. Boundaries, borders, fences, walls, lines telling us who is in and who is out have done serious and significant damage throughout history. Jesus himself broke through the boundary of heaven and earth to begin and live out his boundary breaking ministry. He upset the religious and worldly order as he crossed the boundary from law abiding decency to eating with sinners, hanging out with tax collectors, and touching the untouchable. At his death, the gospel writers tell us the boundary of the temple curtain was torn into two pieces. Normally, I am all for boundaries being broken, if not shattered.

But not always.

In the context of ministry, boundaries are not only healthy but also a must. They have certainly helped Mihee and I survive this complexity of our life together, and this journey, this "odd and wondrous calling."[2]

For clergy couples, and I would say all clergy regardless of marital status, boundaries play an important role. As those called by God to ordained ministry, as we make the transition from seminary to congregation, many times our lives are abruptly on display. In some communities, there is a strangely peculiar interest in the lives of ministers. In one church I served, members would drive by our house to "check it out" and comment on things that were none of their business. I once attended a conference, and the wife of a retired minster told me stories about how church members would comment on the laundry she had hung out to dry in their fenced-in backyard. She couldn't help but resent the members for their unhealthy curiosity and fascination with her and her husband's private life. I assume she is not alone. All clergy, and I am sure professionals in many fields, must decide as their toes approach the limestone chalk separating personal from private just how much they are willing to share with those who sit in the pews.

Cutting Those Lines: Choosing Where They Start and End

> The most important distinction anyone can ever make in their life is between who they are as an individual and their connection with others.
>
> —Anné Linden[3]

We live in an age of Facebook, Twitter, and camera phones. One has to truly be intentional to keep a private life private. And if that decision is made, sometimes congregants will feel hurt, but I think that is okay, once you make that decision for yourself. Often, the biggest challenge in the beginning is just figuring out where those lines are for yourselves, and making sure they are appropriate.

Clergy couples face a unique reality in that the spouse's life is yet another life to navigate in terms of boundaries. Sometimes, the spouses may even differ on how open they want to be with those they serve in their respective communities. In our case, Mihee is generally much more open than me. She has a very active blog, Facebook, Twitter, Pinterest, and other outlets in which she communicates with a high level of honesty, vulnerability, and transparency. I have a blog, but it is infrequently kept current. I have decided that I want to keep a lot of my personal life my own.

Honestly, it has some to do with how much I trust the members of the church that I am serving at the time. While it may sound harsh, the truth is they also have the prerogative to share with me only what is comfortable to them. Presbyterian (and other) clergy also have to deal with the truth that members know exactly what we make in salary, our benefits, and how much vacation time we have each year. Unless they volunteer that information, I don't know what my members make in their line of work, and I certainly do not have a say or vote in the matter. It is potentially an odd paradox. It has taken me a while to get used to the more than public role of the office, where there is an unspoken expectation to maybe know more about my personal history or my opinion on certain political matters. In general, this is not an easy line to navigate in these kinds of relationships. There are simply some things that are off limits. Having children has added another layer of topics that I am comfortable sharing only in my own home. So I put a boundary around them. However, my current congregation consists of many amazing and trustworthy members. They are interested in, but not obsessed with, my personal life. They respect the boundary of work and home, of personal and private. Ironically, it compels me to trust them more. And as a result, I feel closer to them.

Obviously, there are issues and items that overlap for Mihee and me. There are things that we have to deliberately agree upon in terms of what and how much we are going to make public. We've argued about many of these things and coming to a mutual decision is not always easy. But we've decided to err on the side of respect for the other in cases where our spouse has strong feelings. I have agreed to be more open with some things for Mihee's sake. She has honored my wish for privacy in other areas. It's a necessary compromise with no formula that applies to every situation.

Having boundaries with individual church members has been of the utmost importance for us as well. We have both worked with young people of the opposite sex. We have both worked with attractive adults of the opposite sex. Many times those encounters happen when the spouse is not around. There must be a level of trust in the appropriate boundaries we have discussed and agreed upon, and that are in place in documents like the church's sexual misconduct policy. In this case, boundaries are essential. We always share (if possible beforehand) when and where these interactions will take place. Again, building and maintaining trust is vital for clergy couples, or clergy and spouse. If the camera were to flash down to our shoes in these scenes, we've decided that, like Shoeless Joe, we are staying put and not crossing that boundary line into those potentially dangerous grounds. I wish I could say that not much ever happens to give rise to worry in this regard, but unfortunately we saw that it can happen even to the best people.

Crashing through Boundaries: Dealing with
Unusual Relationships

Then I had one of *those* situations.

At one church, a member made sexual advances toward me. He or she offered me expensive gifts. It wasn't a tentative crossing of the professional pastor/member boundary—this person inserted himself or herself into my personal space, and it was emotionally traumatic. My first phone call was to Mihee. I had to share what had happened and to know that she would be there to support me. It was only after talking and sharing this with her that I alerted the appropriate others and sought out colleagues for practical steps going forward. In this case, Mihee was my loving and supportive spouse, not just a colleague in ministry. And that is exactly what I needed from her at the time. While I am not going into much detail here, even divulging this much of that experience in this platform was something we needed to discuss together to make sure we felt it was right.

Most churches have at least one or more members who behave in unhealthy ways. There is always someone who is too needy and/or too opinionated, and who would occupy the entire staff of the church forty hours a week. Not only is this kind of member mentally and emotionally draining, but they also represent another need for boundaries. We've learned that we must create a boundary to safeguard and protect the other. Sharing appropriate information with Mihee has been vital for me. Knowing that she is aware of at least who this needy member is has allowed me to not worry as much. We are able to build and maintain a protective boundary for one another, especially if this member calls the house on a regular basis. We both have a desire to be helpful to our members, even the overly needy ones. Having this boundary lets us remind one another when someone is taking up too much of our time, energy, and emotion. This has been most helpful in my ministry.

In *Field of Dreams*, many boundaries are broken by Shoeless Joe, Moonlight Graham, and others. It makes for a beautiful story, and one that I can't watch without tearing up. The question is posed to Ray Kinsella several times during the movie: "Is this heaven?" His response: "No, it's Iowa." However, at the end of the movie, as healing and reconciliation take place with his deceased father, there is a hint that perhaps it is heaven—or some form of it. And I'm convinced that in the heavenly

Kingdom of God boundaries will indeed be broken. Walls will be torn down, glass ceilings will be shattered, chains will be loosed, and human made limitations will be lifted. While we seek to play our part in building that boundary breaking kingdom, there must be some boundaries in place to allow us to do so. And maybe then we could answer the question posed to Kinsella with "No, but it's on its way."

MIHEE KIM-KORT

After we became ordained in PC (USA) churches, we both fell into ministry with the enthusiasm of fresh, newly minted seminary graduates— wide-eyed and hopeful—and delved into connecting with our churches. We soon discovered the necessity for practical steps in creating healthy and appropriate boundaries with our respective church members. It seemed vitally important to do this when it came to members who were particularly needy or those of the opposite gender, especially since we were not able to be present in each other's church communities. Holding each other gently accountable to those boundaries, and realizing the flexibility of the lines in different situations, was often tricky.

But it took a while for me to get there. Andy seemed instinctively aware of the professional side of ministry, while I continued to hold onto the ideal that being in a community with people meant that there were no fences and no barriers. I realized that this didn't mean that there should *not* be boundaries. Though initially I may appear quiet and observant, as someone who leans toward *E* a little more than *I* on the Myers-Briggs scale, I have never really been known to be a guarded person. Caution? Eh. Not necessary. I threw caution to the wind and off the mountain and anywhere it could not come back to paralyze me. Andy loves to caution me anytime I start to get too excited about any new venture: "You love to jump in with both feet without paying attention to where you might end up."

Being Idealistic: Creating Soft Boundaries

How very good and pleasant it is when kindred live together in unity!

—Psalm 133:1

One of the major differences between Andy and me, which we have discovered and shared many times, is that I see the glass as half full while he sees the glass as half empty. He says I am idealistic, optimistic, and naïve—head in the clouds, rose-colored glasses, optimistic. I see it as a way of being hopeful and open to any possibility. It was impressed on me in seminary that part of the issue in our churches was the lack of hope in worshiping communities. Trust seemed absent. Honesty, transparency, and vulnerability were avoided and even rejected not only by congregation members but also by ministry leaders. Politics was a dirty word, and yet a game that was played by those in privilege. Professionalism and a polished presentation seemed more important than relevance. I desperately wanted to go against the grain of this cultural tendency in churches. I believed that I could facilitate that change and experience a church where genuine community could be experienced by the people through every season.

I had read so much that was formative in my own thinking about community. It was Bonhoeffer's *Life Together*, which I read before seminary, and re-read again early on in my ministry, that inspired me the most. The way he explores the idea of church and what should happen in the gathering is challenging. Bonhoeffer concludes that we are to live as the body of the Church, exercising our gifts to assist the body of believers, and then working through that body to reach out to those who still have not made a commitment to the Christian cause. *But, he emphasized, the way to accomplish this is through unity.* To me this meant eliminating boundaries. When the people of God come together to share their lives openly and freely, accepting each other with a kind of unconditional positive regard, there is a sort of social-spiritual "chemistry" that emerges, and those who come together experience a delightful cohesion and sense of belonging.

> Christian community is like the Christian's sanctification. It is a gift of God which we cannot claim. Only God knows the real state of our fellowship, of our sanctification. What may appear weak and trifling to us may be great and glorious to God. Just as the Christian should not

be constantly feeling his spiritual pulse, so, too, the Christian community has not been given to us by God for us to be constantly taking its temperature. The more thankfully we daily receive what is given to us, the more surely and steadily will fellowship increase and grow from day to day as God pleases.[4]

To me, the basis of these authentic relationships in Christian community was a perspective of our neighbor as exemplified by Christ's own earthly ministry, and the way he saw people. I turned often to C. S. Lewis in *The Weight of Glory*:

> There are no ordinary people. You have never talked to a mere mortal. Nations, cultures, arts, civilizations—these are mortal, and their life is to ours as the life of a gnat. But it is immortals whom we joke with, work with, marry, snub, and exploit—immortal horrors or everlasting splendours. This does not mean that we are to be perpetually solemn. We must play. But our merriment must be of the kind (and it is, in fact, the merriest kind) which exists between people who have, from the outset, taken each other seriously—no flippancy, no superiority, no presumption. And our charity must be real and costly love, with deep feeling for the sins in spite of which we love the sinners—no mere tolerance, or indulgence which parodies love as flippancy parodies merriment. *Next to the Blessed Sacrament itself, your neighbor is the holiest object presented to your senses.* If he is your Christian neighbour, he is holy in almost the same way, for in him also Christ, the glorifier and the glorified, Glory Himself, is truly hidden.[5]

If we all perceived our neighbors in this way, *apart from the normal and conventional societal boundaries*, I believed that our life together in churches would be drastically different. But, in many instances, I felt that I had to take the first step. I would make an effort to be vulnerable, whether it was preaching, teaching, or pastoral. And I saw this openness melt away those walls. Stories would come gushing out over coffee or lunch about struggles with faith, disillusionment with church, stories about marriage and family problems, addictions, difficulties in childhood, financial burdens, and even people's darkest fears and scars. It felt right. It felt like the way God intended for community to be in Christ—and I, too, experienced grace in miraculous ways through these moments.

But the tide turned a bit. This transparency did not always produce the same outcome in every one of my relationships.

Being Realistic: Laying Down Hard Boundaries

I was in my first call. Part of my job description was to help organize a mission trip during which we would work with a family in rural poverty. It would entail painting, cleaning, and some repair in their home, but we would be there for a week with a few other church groups, and it sounded like an amazing opportunity. I was thrilled. We began planning and meeting regularly, and I felt it was a wonderful way to get to know more of the congregation, and not only the youth.

As the week of the trip got closer and our fundraising seemed to intensify each month, I began to hear some grumblings: I was sending too many emails. I ran meetings too long. I wasn't spending enough time on construction work training. I needed to initiate more fundraising events. I continued to hear these kinds of complaints from one particular family, and I started to feel my enthusiasm wane for the trip. Still, my head of staff was completely supportive of my leadership, and he constantly encouraged me to forge ahead. Finally, at one point, near a breaking point for me, I sat down with the one trip participant who was particularly vocal about her dissatisfaction with my leadership. We talked, I shared, she shared, and, in my eyes, I felt that we had broken through some barrier and made a connection. We prayed together, and I left feeling renewed energy.

I could not have been more clueless.

Later that evening I got a call from my head of staff. He had received an email from this participant: "Mihee is not a good leader or pastor. . . . She is obviously and completely unfit to supervise this group. . . . She should not be leading the trip, and I will not be a part of this group unless you prohibit her from going on it. . . . I would be willing to lead the group myself."

I was blindsided. Floored. And completely shocked. I didn't understand how this possibly could have happened to me. Did I not do everything right? I was vulnerable. I had invited her to be the same way. We shared, prayed, and seemed to have crossed over into something new. To say I felt hurt and betrayed would be an understatement.

When Andy and I processed this whole situation together, it happened to be during our vacation. It was always difficult for us to vacation because it seemed like there was usually some kind of drama occurring at one of our churches at the same time. We were in Pittsburgh with Andy's parents, trying to enjoy the sights and sounds of their beloved city and spend time with his grandmother. Of course, we had a hard time being present as I tried to figure out what to do from afar. In between meals, I was on the phone, and while we toured the city, I was emailing and processing with Andy. I could see the strain on his face. It was not only about the boundaries of our family life being crossed by work and this situation—he could see the way it affected me. It was another sort of boundary he felt he could not protect for me, but wanted to for my sake. Our conversations were fraught with heightened sensitivity and, as a result, some misunderstanding and arguments. This situation had crossed many boundaries, and I was not sure it would really produce anything positive.

What ended up happening when I returned from my vacation was that the head of staff asked this person to step down and not participate in the mission trip. She and her mother left the church.

What we hunger for perhaps more than anything else is to be known in our full humanness, and yet that is often just what we also fear more than anything else. It is important to tell at least from time to time the secret of who we truly and fully are . . . because otherwise we run the risk of losing track of who we truly and fully are and little by little come to accept instead the highly edited version which we put forth in hope that the world will find it more acceptable than the real thing.

—Frederick Buechner[6]

Even now when I look back and try to make sense of the situation, I realize perhaps I had held onto an ideal—that as a pastor I could be known in my full humanness and that would somehow be enough. I had made some assumptions. I had been careless. I did not have the foresight to see other possible outcomes. And, most of all, I let work cross over into my home life. I found myself instinctively swinging to the other extreme. I closed myself off as much possible. The boundaries, I realized, were not only for others' sakes but also for my own. And I needed to learn what it would mean to see boundaries as protection for me and my family. But, even though it felt counter to my personality, it was not all negative. *It was also about a distance rooted in trusting that God was already doing the necessary work in the people around me, and I did not need to do everything.* I did not need to be everything. It was not my job or in my call to make everyone a certain way. I was not called to uphold a narrow and individual perspective of living out community.

Being Cautiously Optimistic: Walking the Line

> Stop trying to protect, to rescue, to judge, to manage the lives around you . . . remember that the lives of others are not your business. They are their business. They are God's business . . . even your own life is not your business. It also is God's business. Leave it to God. It is an astonishing thought. It can become a life-transforming thought . . . unclench the fists of your spirit and take it easy.
>
> —Frederick Buechner[7]

At this point, I continue to try to find a manageable balance. What it boils down to now is *priority*. It was a struggle in the beginning for Andy and me to align our priorities. In the beginning, we often discussed the push and pull between marriage and ministry. Growing up in a traditional Korean Presbyterian church, I saw that ministry was clearly a priority over everything, including marriage and family. Although I knew that I should hold my marriage and family life above my vocation, I could not help but do the opposite. I internally justified this view by convincing myself that it was about differentiation, and thriving as an individual *for the sake of my marriage.* I did not want the boundaries between Andy and myself to be blurred, either. I wanted to be the best me—woman, wife, and pastor—possible.

When Andy called me to tell me about his first incident with a parishioner acting truly inappropriately toward him, I was floored. We'd often heard of different stories while in seminary, but they seemed likely abstract examples associated with the polity ordination exam—vaguely real, but did they really happen to ministers? My instinct was to treat the situation as such. I thought about all the professional and ministerial approaches to the situation. And then I realized: *He needs me to be his wife. His companion. His partner. To create a space for him to pour out all his feelings about the situation—whether it involved being a minister or not—and let him process it the way he needed to at the moment, and not even as a professional.* He had been violated by this person, and that kind of trauma required the safety and comfort of a loved one. I knew he would get the right advice and wisdom from his mentors and head of staff, so what he needed from me was simple: a listening ear and encouraging words that he was not at fault. Although it didn't completely change my opinion of boundaries in ministry, it certainly broke through my idealism a little in a way that was important. It was at that moment I had a glimpse of the necessity of boundaries, and not walking naïvely into any situation.

And yet it isn't a simple, linear process. *What I continue to learn is how to walk the line. Those boundaries are important—between me and my work, between myself and my congregation, and, yes, between me and Andy. But the priority in my life—as in, what centers me, grounds me, and sustains my life—is my family life, and my life with Andy.* It is not easy by any means, but it is a worthwhile struggle, and one that ultimately helps me to be a better minister.

AFTERWORDS

> A priest is someone willing to stand between a God and a people who are longing for one another's love, turning back and forth between them with no hope of tending either as well as each deserves. To be a priest is to serve a God who never stops calling people to do more justice and love more mercy, and simultaneously to serve people who nine times out of ten are just looking for a safe place to rest. To be a priest is to know that things are not as they should be and yet to care for them the way they are.
> —Barbara Brown Taylor, *Leaving Church: A Memoir of Faith*[8]

Boundary training is often a requirement for seminarians and ministers in terms of sexual ethics policy. But lines drawn around people are a reality. There are physical lines, emotional and intellectual. The awareness that tangible boundaries are absolutely essential needs genuine verbalization. The propensity of emotions becoming confused or misconstrued in the minister/member relationship will always be a possibility. So, whether those boundaries are spoken (as in policy or institutional process) or unspoken (cultural and traditional ways that safeguard appropriate relationships), they require navigation and intentionality. Yet some may be guidelines, while others are set in stone based on some other past situation or precedent. Either way, they are to be seen and named by communities.

At the same time, some boundaries might need to be broached or broken. How do we know the difference? How do we know which lines we are good to cross (and let others cross) and how do we know which lines are off limits? Are some boundaries more important than others? Can they change over time? The answers to these questions vary according to situation, circumstance, individual decisions, and decisions made together. For example, boundaries set forth in a sexual misconduct policy are standard in many communities and organizations. Those are boundaries in place to protect the parishioner as well as the clergy and staff. However, the boundary around the pulpit or lectern is one that might be broken if your congregation allows and supports laity reading from the Bible, or even preaching on Sunday mornings.

For the minister and his or her spouse and family, it makes good sense to have clear and deliberate conversations regarding personal and potential boundaries with the church community. For instance, Mihee and I just give each other a heads-up when meeting with a member of the opposite sex or if there was a potentially uncomfortable interaction. Openness is not only about parishioners but also between people who are valuable to one's immediate community (parents, children, spouse). This openness helps us to navigate those more fuzzy boundaries, and can assist us in how we might continuously improve and refine those lines, and the reason why we need them.

—AK

CONNECT

- Do you think openness with your congregation leads to vulnerability and could that be a good thing or a harmful thing?
- What boundaries do you have in place and why? What boundaries do you need to strengthen or build? Which boundaries should be crossed or broken?
- Do you trust others right away, giving them the benefit of the doubt? Or do others have to earn your trust? How do you build and maintain trust with your spouse and your congregation?

- Do you think all boundaries apply to all contexts? Or are there some contexts and communities that need more (or less) boundaries than others?

5

COMBINATION

Leading in a Ministry Setting Together

ANDY KORT

> The purpose of relationship is not to have another who might complete you, but to have another with whom you might share your completeness.
>
> —Neale Donald Walsch [1]

Being raised, educated, and now working in a denomination that is a part of the Reformed tradition, I have come to embrace the theological understanding of the Priesthood of All Believers. If you are reading this book, then I assume you have a good handle on what that is, but allow me to humbly offer this simple definition: The Priesthood of All Believers boldly declares that all who believe have a ministry. The priest, pastor, minister, teaching elder, vicar, rector, or any other title for those formally trained and ordained persons are not the only ones charged with doing ministry in Jesus's name. Those in the pews, those who sit around committee tables, who serve coffee and cookies in the fellowship hall, who teach Sunday school and help in the nursery, those who pray, those who give of their time and talents and treasures, those who arrange and deliver flower on Sundays, those who do the millions of little things and the multitude of big things to make the church the Body of Christ at work all have a ministry.

I have known some pastors who are threatened by this premise. They are of the breed that has to do everything, control everything, and have a hand in everything. Some congregations even encourage this and become paralyzed when a pastor is only on vacation or, worse, sabbatical. Churches and pastors can all too easily become codependent on one another. In these cases, a church can't function and falls to pieces if the pastor is not around doing all that needs to be done, from preaching to unclogging toilets. Some clergy don't know what to do if they are not doing, doing, doing something or anything at the church. It is not healthy for either. The health of the pastor-church relationship is largely dependent on how firmly each believes in the Priesthood of All Believers. The Priesthood of All Believers is a wonderful thing for all involved in the church.

Yet it certainly is a challenge to live into when one working with a spouse who is also a clergy.

Intersections: Learning to Share

One of the assumptions of being in a clergy couple is that the couple engages in ministry together. For some, that happens on a daily or weekly basis. For others, like us, it happens on special occasions. Mihee sang a solo, "Be Thou My Vision," at my ordination, and she preached at my most recent installation. I preached at her ordination. Together we have shared, and led, community Thanksgiving worship services. We certainly talk a lot, probably too much, about ministry at home. We are currently embarking on a new ministry initiative involving her work with university students with much overlap with my church. But the place of intersection in our ministries has mostly been on mission trips.

Mihee can talk about our experience combining in ministry serving in the Dominican Republic, while I will share a little about our work together at a church in Boston. As a seminary intern, I almost went to serve a summer at a church in Oregon. Thankfully, God decided to call me to New England, and not the Pacific Northwest. This church in Boston changed my life and my ministry. Not only is the pastor there one of the most loving, gifted, and talented preachers I know, but the community unabashedly embodies a courageous, gracious church by definition—a collection of broken sinners who come together for the worship and work of Jesus Christ. For me, trying to adequately describe this little church in the "Southie" neighborhood is like trying to describe the view while peering into the Grand Canyon. Words and pictures cannot fully capture it. In my mind, it must simply be experienced. That summer in Boston was one of the best summers of my life.

When I graduated from seminary and began working in the suburbs of New York City and the topic of a domestic mission trip came up, I knew exactly where I wanted to take these young Yankee fans—to the home of the Red Sox. So we planned a trip over the summer to Boston. Mihee came with us.

I was so happy to share this community with them. I couldn't wait to take them to Castle Island Park for some greasy fries, burgers, and hot dogs. I looked forward to hopping on the "T" and walking around Harvard Square, playing in Boston Commons, and enjoying some of the other parts of Boston that make it such a great city. I was so eager to have them meet some of the members, the pastor, and my friends from my summer there. Our main mission work there would be to help with the Summer Meals Program. The SMP provides free and nutritious meals (breakfast and lunch) as well as programs like art, music, drama, and sports for many of the underprivileged children of the neighborhood. Think of Vacation Bible School meets YMCA day camp meets art camp—on steroids. It is both crazy and fantastic.

When we finally arrived that July in Boston and settled into our home for our week, the un-air-conditioned church sanctuary, we headed out for some food. I knew that something was off after I stood in line for some long-awaited New England clam chowder, only to have the person in front of me get the last bowl. As I spooned a bite of my second choice, chicken noodle soup, I knew this experience would not be like the romantic vision I had in mind. The lack of clam chowder was not the only disappointment. Looking back, I can see that a lot of the problems on this trip were my fault. At the time, my thinking went something like this: *this is my youth group from my church at a place that I have experienced and feel the most connected to.* Therefore, I felt the need to be in control of almost every detail. I guess I felt that was taking ownership of the situation. Since Mihee was there, and is really good at these kinds of things, I put her in charge of the evening group devotions. It should have been a home run.

As we circled up, sitting in those terribly hard metal folding chairs, she began to lead. Part of her agenda was to ask the youth questions and respond to them as we processed the day and reflected on an appropriate scripture passage. As they offered their responses and reflections, Mihee would begin to answer and keep up the conversation. The youth would listen, hanging on her every word and eager to soak it all in. And then, night after night, I ruined it.

In my excitement as the resident-expert in the Boston experience, I jumped in, interrupted her, and cut her answers short. I began to pontificate about what I thought was important for the group to take away for the night. Basically, I asked her to lead this exercise and activity, and then I hijacked it and took it from her. And I did it again and again. That's what is so disappointing. I should have known better. Actually, I did know better. Mihee and I talked about it (a lot) during that trip. Even though she vented and told me that I "talk too much," it didn't register right away. I think what didn't sink in was the reality that I was unintentionally usurping her authority as a pastor, a leader, an advisor, and someone with her own authentic voice. I felt that my voice and experience was the only one worth considering. I preached value of the Priesthood of All Believers, but I was very quick to practice something altogether different. At the time, it seemed as if I wanted to be there by myself.

Intersections: Sharing to Lead Well

Along the way, I learned an important lesson as a young, fresh-out-of-seminary pastor: ministry is not about me. I also learned another good lesson: ministry is often best done in combination.

Then he went about among the villages teaching. He called the twelve and began to send them out two by two.

—Mark 6:7

The concept of Jesus sending the disciples out two by two hit me like a four-by-four. Ministry together with others has a strong biblical basis— Jesus models and instructs in this way. It has always amazed me that this God of ours chooses to engage us in ministry when it would probably be a lot easier if God just did it all for us. While God in fact does do "it all" for us, God still involves people like me, Mihee, and countless others. None of us can truly go about the villages teaching alone. There are too many snares and traps along the way. On our own, we are too weak, or, as Calvin might say, we are too depraved. We need the extra set of eyes and ears, as well as the additional thoughts, gifts, skills, and wisdom of others. We need someone else to keep us honest. Even in my time as a solo pastor, I found that ministry is meant to be shared with others. Elders, deacons, and the laity have gifts that are beyond my repertoire. If my ministry were to flourish in any way, it must be in combination with the ministry of others. Unless someone has a passion or a penchant for burn-out, they will undoubtedly be better off combining in ministry with others. I think this is why God has called us into community and something called "the church."

In her sermon "The Open Yoke,"[2] based on Matthew 11:25–30, Barbara Brown Taylor reminds us that there are two kinds of yokes, both used by people all around the world. One is the single kind that seems very efficient. By placing a single pole, or yoke, across one's shoulders, a person can carry much on their own. A bucket of water attached to each end of the pole is a common example of this kind of yoke. And it works fine, but after a while, the one carrying the burden of the work gets too tired to continue. Their shoulders and back hurt. They eventually may become too tired to go on working. The other kind of yoke is one in which the burden of the work is shared equally. The work is just as hard, but because it requires another worker, the labor is divided, as one can ease up some while the other pulls. As Taylor writes, "They can take turns bearing the brunt of the load; they can cover for each other without ever laying their burden down because their yoke is a shared one. They have company all day long, and when the day is done both may be tired but neither is exhausted, because they are a team." This second shared yoke is clearly the better kind—and I needed to learn how to pick it up.

The following summer we headed back to Boston for another week. Once again Mihee came with us. This time was different—better. This time, as we genuinely combined our ministries, the word "amazing" does not even begin to describe the week. Relationships were formed and strengthened, and Mihee was no longer the newbie. She was without question a leader, an equal leader. The more I reflect on it, she was never really the tag-along chaperone. The difference was more with me and my willingness to be in combination with her in this ministry. What I found out was that she actually makes me better. We complemented one another and painted a more complete picture for the overall experience. I was good at the details and the organization, the planning and decision making. She excelled in the moments of downtime and fun activities. She made the trip easier since she was willing to do some of those things that I really wasn't excited about, and vice versa. But I also think that, while I was finally getting how she operates, she was beginning to see how I operate in a ministry setting, too.

As the years since that summer have rolled on, we've settled into a better way of operating together. I have settled into that place. I have had to learn to put down some pride and some ego that may have been rooted in insecurity. I have picked up a joy in watching her, and others, do the work of the gospel, the work to which we are called to share . . . *together*. What I have found is the more I am willing to combine my gifts with hers (and others), the better it is, the better it feels, the better it turns out. When the believers claim their share of the priesthood together ministry happens, the good news is shared, and lives get changed. More than likely, it sometimes is the life of the one doing the ministry.

And, oh yes, during that second trip to Boston I did get my clam chowder. It was delicious.

MIHEE KIM-KORT

In the beginning when Andy and I had just gotten married, we began to talk about the possibility of doing ministry together in a church setting, and of course, we had on the proverbial rose-colored glasses. We dreamed about driving into work together listening to NPR or sports radio. We would be able to work right down the hall from each other. We could schedule meetings around coffee or lunch dates. We might share sermon and liturgy ideas, and possibly do more creative programs. It sounded really ideal.

Except that we had no idea what we were talking about at the moment. Being so different in personality from each other wouldn't magically disappear in a work setting. It had to do with more than whether we like wearing stoles in worship (he does not, and I do), with traditional versus contemporary music, with our preferences for a lot of liturgy or hardly any at all, or a screen in the sanctuary or not.

Andy is the *Other.*

I encountered this language of the *Other* during my undergraduate and seminary coursework, but it wasn't until I started to work in ministry that I felt the tensions of being the *Other.* Foreign. Strange. Exotic. Thankfully, I wasn't alone. I had a community of women and women of color to engage these issues with me within a theological and postcolonial context.

However, it was surprisingly in marriage I truly had to confront the *Other* by waking up every day next to it in the morning hogging all the blankets and two-thirds of our queen-sized bed. But I am the *Other* to him. In a somewhat similar fashion to the old adage "men are from Mars and women are from Venus," we often jokingly lament that there is no one more foreign to us than the other. I am still amazed about so much in his personality. His intensity during his favorite teams' games. His romantic obsession with our dog. His constant need to fix all my "problems." His love of cozy, small spaces when he's 6'3". The strangeness is based not just on gender generalizations but also on who he is simply as a human being. Even after all these years, he remains a mystery to me. A good one. A gracious one.

This would circle back to inform my own identity and calling in so many ways.

See the Other: Confrontation and Being Uncomfortable

> I emphasize in it [my Orientalism] accordingly that neither the term Orient nor the concept of the West has any ontological stability; each is made up of human effort, partly affirmation, partly identification of the Other.
>
> —Edward W. Said[3]

I had only been on one international mission trip before leading a group from the church that was my second call. While I made the rookie mistake of jumping into this position trying to start a new program almost immediately, fifteen people signed up for a work trip to the Dominican Republic during my first summer. Despite the bumps in the road—seeking Session approval amid questions of liability, garnering both emotional and financial support, and encouraging participants to trust me as their leader even though they really did not know me—we made it down there.

For ten days we were with a local community to be extra hands and backs to build their village church, leading their VBS program and other children's activities, and beginning to develop long-term relationships.

I was a nervous wreck.

But I was great at hiding it. I needed to hide it. I told myself they depended on me to hide it. Despite not knowing a lick of Spanish, and never leading an international mission trip before, and feeling so uncertain about all the paperwork, passports, pesos, and planning, I threw myself into it with a desperation and ferocity almost of a wild animal finding itself backed into a corner by a predator. That predator was fear and insecurity about my leadership ability, worry about what the participants would think of my leadership, and how I needed so much to prove myself at so many levels. Internally, all I could focus on was my inadequacy.

That first evening we stepped into the community's little church for the first worship service. The dirt floor was lined with broken wooden benches, a makeshift podium for a lectern, and one speaker plugged into a small electronic piano.

I was broken wide open. A single, dim light bulb hung from the ceiling, but the presence of God was so bright and warm, welcoming and true. The music clashed and was unfamiliar, blocks and wheelbarrows were the only vestments to decorate the space, the liturgy virtually nonexistent and the stole the *pastora* wore was nothing but a white hand towel she used to swat at flies and mosquitos. But it was home. All that desperation fell away. I saw myself in the people that surrounded me, both white and black. I saw myself in the *mezcla*—the mud and rock mixture used as cement for the bricks of the walls—and the buckets being passed from one hand to another. I saw myself in the trees longing for rain and sun, even the children that played so freely and joyfully. All this because of the light not only from that small, dim bulb hanging in the church sanctuary but also from God's Spirit so clearly present. The brief downpour of rain every day, the small cups of water handed out every hour, the buckets of water mixed in with the cement mixture—it was like being baptized all over again.

It felt like that all week. Moments of epiphany around every corner and in every conversation about language and culture, spirituality and faith, God's presence showing up in unexpected ways, receiving incredible ministry and affirmation from both Americans and Dominicans, and being humbled over and over again. It was so much more than I had ever felt before in my life. I saw so much.

I couldn't wait to tell Andy about it all.

Embrace the Other: Compassion and a New Posture

> Hospitality means primarily the creation of free space where the stranger can enter and become a friend instead of an enemy. Hospitality is not to change people, but to offer them space where change can take place. It is not to bring men and women over to our side, but to offer freedom not disturbed by dividing lines.
>
> —Henri J. M. Nouwen[4]

When I got home I found I needed time to process. Andy and I went out to dinner, but I was faltering and stumbling over words adequate enough to describe the experience. Andy had gone to Nicaragua with a group from his first call, and I remember feeling so disconnected from his stories, trying to imagine what it would be like to be there. Much as words felt lacking, we both were in awe that after this kind of experience it was undeniable that a change happens in the way we interact with others, even in the way we might sit, stand, and, certainly, see the world.

The following year Andy and a group from his church joined us. Andy and I had led mission trips together before, but this was the first time I was the lead, and it was in an international setting. This being the second year, and I had already gone back down twice on weekend leaders' trips during the year, I felt much more at ease. Even the fundraising felt like less of a burden, and it is normally the biggest cause of stress. As Andy and I began to coordinate the minor logistics of transportation and luggage, passports and insurance card copies, I started to feel anxious again. Our times leading the mission trips in Boston together weren't easy, and I couldn't help but remember how every night that week ended in tears (mostly from me) and long, hard conversations working through numerous frustrations. In some ways, that was much more exhausting than the actual mission work. I wondered if we would have to revisit these issues, since it had been a while.

As the day of our departure arrived, I started to feel a tension in my shoulders. I could sense that he was also stressed. His church members were late for our departure to the airport. Being really sensitive to how he was feeling, I also started to feel stressed. In private moments we were snippy to each other. I wonder if being at the church at 3 a.m. had something to do with it. Finally, when his group showed up and we got to the airport, we were able to relax a little, talk out the schedule, and connect with the adult leaders. We were on our way.

When we stepped out of the airport, the familiar Caribbean air gathered me up in a lovely embrace. I normally abhor humidity, but the sea, sun, and sky wrapped me in calm and joy. It would be a good week, I was sure of it. I would remember the lessons I learned from the previous summer about the compassion I received from the Dominicans. The best image I still carry around, and made sure to hold up in my mind, was the sight of a Dominican child wiping the sweat off my face with a bandana during a break in the middle of one of the hottest days. I realized that my most important role was not to be a leader but a follower—to follow in the footsteps of Jesus in this little child and extend compassion with both Dominicans and Americans. And even my husband, Andy, no matter what the situation.

Identify with the Other: Combining and Intersecting

> If everyone helps to hold up the sky, then one person does not become tired.
>
> —Askhari Johnson Hodari[5]

> The point of marriage is not to create a quick commonality by tearing down all boundaries. . . . A merging of two people is an impossibility, and where it seems to exist, it is a hemming-in, a mutual consent that robs one party or both parties of their fullest freedom and development. But once the realization is accepted that even between the closest people infinite distances exist, a marvelous living side-by-side can grow up for them, if they succeed in loving the expanse between them, which gives them the possibility of always seeing each other as an immense sky.
>
> —Rainer Maria Rilke[6]

Andy and I would go back many more times with our groups. Even though there was also some kind of stress to manage together, we eventually found a rhythm. But during 2010, when I was pregnant with the twins, he insisted I stay home. "Are you kidding me?!" I responded. "This is my baby. My project. And my body. I know what I can and cannot handle."

We went back and forth trying to come to some sort of agreement as the weeks rushed by. Finally, we came to a compromise that neither of us liked at all. I would come toward the second half of the trip. He would rather I not go at all, and I, of course, felt like it was necessary for me to be there.

When I finally got to Santo Domingo, I was relieved but felt so out of it. It's hard and awkward to enter into a situation where you've missed so many interactions and stories, so many moments and inside jokes, and so many hours of grueling work. It upset me. And I blamed Andy for it. At the work site he admonished me to take it easy and not strain myself for the sake of the pregnancy. Our roles had shifted this time, and it caused conflict. I was used to being in charge and coordinating every detail. But he had stepped up in my absence, and it felt like he was making all the decisions, from praying before the work day to coordinating the Dominicans on the worship services. At one point, I had simply said, "Andy, before we start the day we need to pray with the Dominicans," and he gave me a look. Later, in the "privacy" of a corner in the church building, we went back and forth. Loudly. Two trip participants, a father and daughter, were nearby taking a water break, clearly within hearing range; normally I would have been embarrassed, but this time I didn't care.

"I'm going to go home. It's obvious that you don't need me here!" I said, fighting back tears. "You've apparently got everything under control, and I shouldn't say anything or give any input, and anyway, I've missed out on so much already, and all you're going to do is be negative toward me and treat me like a child for the rest of the week, so . . . screw you!" I actually used words that I would often tell the youth to not use around me.

We didn't talk for the rest of the day. Though we had come to a tentative reconciliation later, the next few days seemed to go by almost too slowly, and I was ready to get back home. But I was so heartbroken that this would be how I would leave my last trip to the Dominican Republic.

Later, when we reflected on this trip, we discovered that the main point of contention was the blurred line between being each other's colleague *and* spouse. We were pretty good at separating the two in most situations. But we realized that it was because we were rarely in situations like this together.

However, taking a cue from the Dominican pastors Juan José and Adriana, who weren't tied to titles and roles, I couldn't help wonder if that would translate in our context. Though the *pastora* was clearly the organizing leader, and she was an important fixture in the community because of her ability to provide both spiritual and physical care as a medical doctor, Juan José had a role, too, as a counselor, worship leader, and a symbol of strength. Still, they were interchangeable. They seemed comfortable in the fluidity of their roles. Later, we would learn that, tragically, Juan José suffered from a terminal illness, a type of cancer, and would refuse medical treatment, turning instead to prayer and fasting. He passed away in 2012. It was clear the community was suffering a huge loss. I can only imagine what the *pastora* was going through herself. Not only did she lose a partner in ministry, but she also lost a partner in life.

I wondered what ultimately was the bigger loss for them. Now she was carrying the burden of ministry by herself, but also the burden of providing medical care, teaching, parenting, and simply living. It's hard to delineate where being a spouse ends and colleague begins when one is married to someone of the same profession. But I understand a little now that when Andy fought me on the timing of my departure to the Dominican Republic, it was not as a colleague, but as a worried spouse. Likewise, in the Dominican Republic, when he tried to convince me to take it easy on the work, it was as a concerned spouse. But when we argued about it then, I perceived it as a criticism toward me as a colleague. When I suggested something, it was as a colleague, but it may have been received as a spouse. Our communication was entrenched in the assumptions of each role, and we were missing what the other was trying to say out of love and concern.

All this is to say, there is no easy way to be together as spouses and colleagues. Truly, context is everything, but we have to work consciously at making sure the overarching context is our covenant to one another. But, like everything else we are finding out about life itself, there's no blueprint or magic formula to marriage, and definitely not to ministry together. Witnessing the work of the Dominicans, and the work of the church members together, I was moved by how much overlap there was in their community, and how much they shared their lives. The church was more than a place of worship, and even more than a community center of programs—it was a place where people lived together, struggled together, fought and created, and faced life and death.

Those boundaries between church and neighborhood, ministry and marriage were porous. And we saw in the Dominican community, and in our own experience, that while there wasn't a perfect or ideal situation that would make these relationships easy, it made it richer. More overlap—more possibilities of overlap, more places of intersection (though often wrought with some kind of conflict or confrontation)—would make for a richer connection. We could be spouse and colleague at the same time, and even though they wouldn't always be "equal" in the way we would normally measure or quantify it, our work would constantly be shifting in ways that would hopefully be necessary to the specific situation. Sometimes he would do more, and sometimes I would do more. Sometimes he would be in the public more, and sometimes I would take on that role more. Submission had a whole new meaning, and, in fact, it seemed to mean flexibility more than anything else.

Much of this reflection has come out of understanding God's encounter with us in terms of radical reconciliation—that is, reconciliation with the least likely person, someone foreign, an enemy, a Samaritan like in the Parable of the Good Neighbor. In this case, there has to be acknowledgment and an embrace of difference, conflict, hostility, and unfamiliarity, a true and real encounter with the "Other" and the "Stranger," for community—relationships in every context—to reach the depths of this reality. The wider the gap, the more unlikely the connection, the more hostile the history, the more barriers and the higher the walls—the more sweet and beautiful—the wonder of the occurrence of connection and life together.

I had no idea that the Dominicans would teach me not only about ministry but also about navigating the waters of marriage together, serving together in ministry—always imperfectly, and always miraculously.

AFTERWORDS

"What do you want in a woman, in life?" I thought a moment. . . . The Rangers . . . we began to describe one another in a few simple words: El es muy bueno para cabalgar el rio. Meaning, "He'll do to ride the river with." In Texan, it means, "I'd trust him with my life." I scratched my head. "I want someone to ride the river with."

—Charles Martin[7]

There is a funny scene from the television show *The Office* with Oscar giving an interview. It takes place in the context of Jim and Michael both serving as co-managers of their paper company as they struggle with power and other dynamics. Oscar looks at the camera and says, "Look it doesn't take a genius to know that every organization thrives when it has two leaders. *[shakes head]* Go ahead, name a country that doesn't have two presidents. A boat that sets sail without two captains. Where would Catholicism be, without the [two] popes?"

It is a humorous quote that leads one to believe that fundamentally there must be only one person in charge. One pope. One captain. One president. One manager. One leader. But is that always true in ministry? Maybe.

But then again, maybe not. While I think we would both admit that doing things on our own might be easier, we would also suggest that God does not always call people to what is easiest. No one in their right mind goes into ministry because it is easy or they want things to be easy. Right? Instead, we have come to believe that shared ministry, when possible, is the easiest, not because the tasks and responsibilities are less burdensome, but because God meant for us to share the burden. Admittedly, there are many times when sharing ministry is not easy, either. We all have different thoughts, opinions, and ideas about what we would like to see happen or maybe we struggle with someone else. As those conversations play themselves out into real-life decisions and actions, sometimes someone gets disappointed. But that is true in any relationship or organization with more than one person.

I keep coming back to the call of Moses to lead the people out of the horrible grip of the Pharaoh. Only God did not call Moses alone. He also called Aaron. Why? Because there were some parts of the job, essential parts such as speaking, that Moses did not particularly like or feel equipped or able to do. So God called and sent someone who was much more eloquent alongside of him. Does Moses get much of the credit? Yes. Did Moses do a lot of the heavy lifting? Sure. But could he have done it alone, without the help of Aaron? That is debatable. All we have to go on is the reality that they went together and called together, working together and liberating the captives together. No one can doubt there is something unique in the witness of God's people leading together.

—AK

CONNECT

- How do you identify the gifts and skills of another?
- How do you make room for them in your ministry or leadership?
- If those gifts overlap with yours, how do you negotiate the sometimes tricky task of collaboration?
- How do you encourage others to make space for the gifts you bring to ministry or leadership? What are those gifts?

6

COOPERATION

Raising Children as Partners and Pastors

MIHEE KIM-KORT

Parenthood is not for the faint of heart.

Before we got married, we had talked some about having children. But not much. It was just a given that we would have children, and when it came to that point, we would work out what our full-time careers would look like while raising them. Of course, as has often been noted, "The best-laid plans of mice and men often go astray."[1] But when those plans were not even laid, expectations and assumptions still became disappointments, especially since they were internalized for years. Our parents obviously had children. Our cousins and friends were having children. Most of our culture, particularly in church culture, said in so many unspoken words that children were the inevitable next step; it was just a matter of when, *and why were we taking so long*? We knew raising children would provide some challenges, but actually producing children? Infertility was a whole other world.

And then when our babies did finally grace our lives, few words truly described the changes that happened to us as a couple. Gut-wrenching. Mind-numbing. Life-altering. These words hardly do it justice, but they come close. Anything along the lines of military boot camp, backpacking in the wilderness, and running marathons would provide adequate language. And while there are piles of stories sky high about the wonder and magic of becoming parents, it seemed only in recent history, with the widespread availability of social media, that we heard parenting was much more than cuddling with a squishy newborn while gazing into each other's eyes, and that it was, in fact, one of the most difficult endeavors we would enter into as a couple.

Still, we would never say anything less than that these children have captured our hearts. And we are grateful for this call to family.

Partners: Primary vs. Secondary Caregiver

> Each suburban wife struggled with it alone. As she made the beds, shopped for groceries, matched slipcover material, ate peanut butter sandwiches with her children, chauffeured Cub Scouts and Brownies, lay beside her husband at night—she was afraid to ask even of herself the silent question—"Is this all?"
>
> —Betty Friedan[2]

The notion of primary versus secondary came up as we discussed a leave of absence with both of our churches. Fortunately, we each had the opportunity to take maternity *and* paternity leave. This parity was a blessing and a wonderful expression of how far the church has come in supporting clergy and their families. Although my church did not have a maternity policy technically in place, the personnel committee worked quickly and fairly to provide me with support, despite the news that our family was leaving to follow God's call to Andy to a church in Bloomington. Without this time of transition into having the twins, I am not sure we would have survived the first two months of their lives.

When we moved to Bloomington, and after the dust settled a bit, I began to examine what it really meant to be the primary caregiver to the children. According to Wikipedia, it is "the person who takes primary responsibility for someone who cannot care fully for themselves. It may be a family member, a trained professional or another individual. Depending on culture there may be various members of the family engaged in care. The concept can be important in attachment theory as well as in family law, for example in guardianship and child custody."[3]

Even though it was a legal designation, it felt like much more. In day-to-day terms, I know it meant I am the one that will be the most present with the children on a regular basis. This meant feeding, changing, helping them nap/sleep, and playing with them. It also meant that I would be "on"—clocked in and laboring away. *Constantly*. The hours started to bleed into each other so that it really did not matter if it was day or night—only how many hours until their next nap. I remember snoozing on the couch early in the morning while the twins slept in their bouncy seats, and Andy had come down to get ready to go to church. It was a Sunday morning. And it felt like he lost all sensitivity toward volume, since it sounded like he was slamming all the cabinet doors shut. I woke up, the babies stirred and started to fuss, and I hissed in my loudest quiet voice, "PLEASE DO NOT SLAM THE CABINET DOORS!!! The babies just fell asleep, and this is all I wanted from them, and they are finally asleep, and you woke all of us up, and . . . I hate my life!!!"

Needless to say, Andy was rattled. He left for work pretty quickly, and I sat in the dark, bouncing the chairs, wondering how I got here. Is this what I signed up for when I became a parent?

As the primary caregiver, did it mean that this would be my only job? My only vocation? Would I carry the bulk of this work? Somehow it became more than work but a fundamental change in my being. Becoming a parent was viscerally different from anything else. I was no doubt madly in love with these babies. I stared at them every possible second. I constantly held their little hands looking at fingers that couldn't possibly one day hold mine back. I wanted to freeze them in this moment forever, so they wouldn't have to face peer pressure, body image issues, and stupid boys or girls breaking their hearts. I believed that every single movement and facial twitch was an expression of the Divine.

Yet fear colored every moment. If I was driving around with the babies, at every four-way intersection I paused for much longer than necessary. Images of a huge Ford truck barreling through without stopping and t-boning my little Subaru plagued me. If I laid the babies down on the carpet, I walked on eggshells, dreading the possibility that I might accidentally step on someone's head. If I was in the grocery store with the babies, I steered clear of anyone coughing for fear of some unknown tropical, rare disease that might infect them. I became totally and completely irrational in my fear, and it sometimes paralyzed me. This was on top of being thoroughly numb from pure exhaustion.

It took a little time to realize that I was not the only one.

Andy was experiencing his own trauma in a way. Giving up control over his schedule, his routines, and almost everything was a lot more difficult than he anticipated in the beginning. Balancing acceptance of this new life with work while trying to be optimistic for my sake but not overly enthusiastic in order to be sensitive to me and my loss—it was arduous to negotiate daily. Realizing our marriage would never be the same, and that I would take a while to get back to "normal," was also something that blindsided us. I could see that strain in his eyes. *While it felt like the bulk of the work for our family fell on me, I started to see how unfair it was to see it that way and realized that while I was working so hard caring for the children, Andy was doing his part for them as well, and he was caring for me.*

I had to let go of set job descriptions. In our marriage, any hint of hierarchy in these roles would lead to a slippery slope. The roles became unhelpful and unnecessary, and in some ways created resentment. For some perhaps this structure is comforting, but for Andy and me, especially me, I needed to see that I still possessed some agency. Bottom line, we learned to share the load in a way that allows for fluidity in our roles. Most mornings Andy unloads the dishwasher and starts breakfast for the twins. I usually take on the bath at night. But this also can change. Sometimes there are meetings. Or last-minute pastoral visitations. Or college student gatherings. We adjust and work it out. Flexibility is the new norm, and communication nurtures and maintains it. There is simply no way to have a neat blueprint for who is going to do or give up what at all times to make this family life sustainable. Bonnie J. Miller-McLemore writes, "The recovery of sacrifice entails seeing it as a central practice in a cycle of gift-exchange, in which giving does not result in loss but rather nurtures communion, mutuality, and interdependence." Sacrifice is not the height and epitome of love. Sacrifice stands in service of mutuality. [4]

This perspective on sacrifice helped me to reframe my vocation in such a way that I saw I was not losing or lacking but part of something much bigger. *To compare or compete, to keep track of or quantify the daily sacrifices, only cuts away at the roots that tie us together.* Because, essentially, we both make sacrifices.

We are both primary caregivers.

Partners: Pursuing Each Other

Even if I'm setting myself up for failure, I think it's worth trying to be a mother who delights in who her children are, in their knock-knock jokes and earnest questions. A mother who spends less time obsessing about what will happen, or what has happened, and more time reveling in what is. A mother who doesn't fret over failings and slights, who realizes her worries and anxieties are just thoughts, the continuous chattering and judgment of a too busy mind. A mother who doesn't worry so much about being bad or good but just recognizes that she's both, and neither. A mother who does her best, and for whom that is good enough, even if, in the end, her best turns out to be, simply, not bad.

—Ayelet Waldman[5]

Becoming a pastor and then a parent is an ego-killer. In my life, nothing continues to humble me time and time again. As a pastor, my days feel full of minute and impossible decisions, and constant second-guessing. *Should I have . . . ? Would I have . . . ? What if . . . ?* This was the most obvious overlap in motherhood and ministry. In caring for the children, I constantly wonder if I should be doing something else whether it is earning more income or doing more arts and crafts with them.

Thankfully, I would not go this alone.

One of the reasons we made the decision to follow God's call to Bloomington for Andy's position was the desire to be in church together on Sunday mornings with our children. We had never really experienced this at all, and having children made sharing a community on Sundays much more urgent. What I did not anticipate at all was how trying it would be for me to sit in the pews with them alone Sunday after Sunday while Andy worked and led worship. Although the church community surrounded us with much love and encouragement, it was still a lonely endeavor. What complicated it even more was constantly facing in Andy's presence in the pulpit what I had given up in Easton—pastoral identity, church community, and an important livelihood.

Needless to say, we had countless conversations about my struggle to accept the reality that I could not have it all. I knew I wanted to stay at home with them for at least the first year. I knew that moving to Bloomington would mean likely not having a call. I knew that eventually I would want to work in some capacity again.

The middle-of-the-night hours were spent checking who else was up on Facebook, scouring parenting blogs, and writing emails to mom-friends lamenting this season and asking every possible question about child development and care. One email response still sticks with me now.

When my mind finally turned from the children to Andy, I mentioned in passing my worry about how having children would impact our marriage, and the feeling that we were two ships passing in the night, where the only time we would interact would be to lob cannonballs at each other from our own decks. It felt like we fought more than talked or listened to each other.

This friend wrote back a number of little nuggets, including this one: *Don't worry about the marriage right now.* This caught me off guard. I thought to myself, "We are on the verge of killing each other most days, or else we are too tired to say or do anything at all. Is it a good idea to not worry about it?"

I read through it again, over and over, and finally saw the words *right now.*

It struck me. This is a temporal season prone to change much like anything and everything else in our lives. She was confident that we had a strong relationship and that we would get through it, and what we should do now was focus on day-to-day survival. The children's survival. The boxer dog, Ellis, and her survival. Our survival. There would be time for the "marriage"—as in, all the things we used to do as a couple—later. This was freeing and helped ease my anxiety.

She was right. When we started to lean into the routine of naps, diapers, and "meals," or Andy's work weeks and meeting schedules, and surrendered to the constant reality of interruptions, it helped us to be open to other ways of connecting with each other again. We would watch episodes of shows that were new to us after the twins went down for the night. Instead of dates, we had breakfasts, and even celebrated an anniversary at a favorite restaurant for brunch. We were too tired for date nights anyway, but when we were able to leave the twins for more than two hours because many church members volunteered to be with them, we could go out for the occasional dinner or drink. We took advantage of the Kids' Night In once a month, so we could grab a quick, early supper. *And our being together made more and more sense, and we remembered not only how much we love each other but also how much we enjoy each other.*

Even so I vacillated between bucking against cultural pressures to be the perfect and willing stay-at-home mom and embracing this as an opportunity to experience and live into a faithfulness. I tried more to frame this as the latter. *There were countless occasions for learning about pa-*

tience, kindness, and gentleness, which were all virtues I needed to culti-
vate in my life. And not only with the children, but even more so with
Andy. I was living and learning what it meant to not fixate over every
little detail and tasks needing to be done a certain way. To see how much
the sarcastic words I said over and over again were detrimental to both of
us. To see how little acts that were thought out and intentional went a
long way. To see how this whole life together is made all the more better
with honesty and hope—and with each other.

After all, we are on the same team.

ANDY KORT

There was a moment that clarified this need for solidarity with each other.
One day last summer we were at a local park. It is big and beautiful and
our city's version of Central Park. Desmond and Anna were about six
months old on this particular day. As we always did, we placed them in
the bucket swings for infants. We pushed; they laughed. The sun was
shining, our kids were happy, and it was great to be out of the house. It
was one of those romantic moments I imagined having kids would be
like. However, being at a public park means that you might encounter the
public. We live in a university town with a lot of educated and enlight-
ened people. Most of the time, this is fantastic and a reason why we enjoy
living here. However, it can also be obnoxious.

A father also of twins approached us and struck up a conversation. As
we were dressed in dirty blue jeans and crusty T-shirts, we noted that he
was sharply dressed. We talked about the normal blah, blah, blah nothing-
ness of conversations that hovers on the surface. He then asked a question
that still annoys us to this day: "So how many languages will your children speak? Mine can speak four." He went on to prophesy that absolutely no child will have any semblance of success in life if he or she cannot
speak multiple languages. Well, my parents must be total failures, and I
must be a very hopeless sap, because I can really only speak English. This
guy went on and on about languages and Montessori and the global
marketplace and how apparently his children would be fast-tracked to
Harvard and then on to international greatness.

I wanted to kick him.

We often make fun of and joke about this guy. We do see him in town, since he works at a popular establishment. And maybe he is right. Maybe Desmond and Anna would be better off if we had them speak multiple languages, potty-trained before three, playing a sport by four, and in a fancy private school. We do hope to teach them some Korean along the way, but they were six months old when he asked us that question. They were not even really making any sounds that resembled any words. I'm not even sure they were sitting up on their own at that point. Even if his point has some validity, the fact that he felt the desire to walk up to new parents he had never met before and offer this make-or-break advice about linguistic ability is what makes me shake my head.

Thinking of this now, what stands out to me the most was that he was alone at the park with his kids. I was there with my wife and partner, with Mihee, and even though we would later trade off and take the kids solo, at this moment, all that mattered was that we were together and what Mihee and I thought and wanted for our children.

Becoming Parents: More than Sacrifice

Sometimes when God answers prayers, even prayers for something we really want, it can turn your world upside down in ways that are not always pleasant. A few years ago I visited a friend in Dallas for a long weekend. It was great to stay with him, his wife, and get to know his two young girls as they introduced me to the Lone Star State. On the last night before I departed, we prayed together in his kitchen. This is not something I normally do when I visit friends, but at the time and in that moment it was the right thing. I prayed, my friend prayed, and then his wife prayed. For the life of me I do not remember my words, or even my friend's words. However, I clearly remember his wife praying for "Andy and Mihee to have children."

As those words left her lips and made their way to God, I opened my eyes because I was surprised to hear them. But they were words that many months later I would lift to God time and time again. Becoming parents was something that eluded us a while. We had a five-year plan. After we got married, we would do our thing for the first five years of marriage. We would get to know one another and settle into this new way of life. We would get established in our careers. We would have fun and do all of the things people told us to do before we had kids. And then year five turned into year seven. Still, no kids.

I had no idea actually conceiving children would be this hard. There were months that felt like roller-coaster rides of emotions and expectations. Hopes sung to the skies and then crumbled to the ground after another negative pregnancy test. Scheduling times for intimacy took its toll on our marriage and impacted our jobs, as our minds were constantly on this extra chore and obligation. In some ways, I almost preferred committee meetings to our "family" meetings. Sundays became difficult, especially for Mihee, because of baptisms, Cradle Roll Sunday, and Mother's Day. I hated seeing her so burdened by this struggle, and not being able to alleviate it in any way.

And so sacrifice took on a new meaning. *We had to surrender our timelines. We had to surrender our schedules. We had to surrender our expectations.* No matter how difficult, we kept trying and hoping, believing that it was meant for us, and that if it wasn't, we would soon find out.

As the years began to turn, our prayers, or mine at least, had an increasing sense of both anguish and longing. After a very up-and-down year full of fear, trembling, and the apprehension that Mihee could not bear children, God answered those prayers: Mihee got pregnant. Proving God has a sense of humor, she was pregnant with twins.

Like everyone else who becomes first-time parents, we dove right into it. I do not know if I am alone in this, but I had a very sentimental idea of what was to come. As I said earlier, sometimes when God answers prayers it can turn everything upside down. My vision of Desmond coming out of the womb able to throw a ball and Anna immediately wanting to climb into my lap was quickly and rudely replaced by Desmond's incessant colicky crying and Anna's general newborn ability to do nothing.

One of the many things people would say to us before the twins came was some version of "Get as much sleep as you can now!" I mostly laughed it off because I had no concept of what was to come. And did it ever come. So did the never-ending cycle of washing bottles, wiping butts, struggling with the swaddling, and my inability to figure out how to buckle the car seats. But, mostly, it was the lack of sleep that began to chip away at us. It was a revelation just how much sleep we would sacrifice in the first year of their lives. *We had to surrender not only our usual sleep but also to the physical toll on our bodies, mentally and emotionally.*

The twins were born during an interesting time. About two months before they were born I accepted a new call at a church in Indiana. We were scheduled to move when they were eight weeks old. I do not recommend this to anyone considering a move. But somehow, mostly because of the grace of our faith communities, we made it work.

With the move to my new church came more responsibilities. But it was different from my last calls when I was able to do anything and be anywhere necessary without worrying about my wife and children. *So this meant surrendering to my usual transition into ministry.* This meant more time at work, more stress at work, more work to bring home with me. At the same time, I was keenly aware there was the additional burden of knowing that Mihee gave up a job she loved at a church she loved at the time. It reminded me that she sacrificed multiple opportunities to pursue a PhD. I quickly learned not to come home excitedly talking about the new restaurant I went to for lunch with a parishioner and the great coffee shop only blocks from the church.

Becoming Parents: More than Work

> I don't remember who said this, but there really are places in the heart you don't even know exist until you love a child.
>
> —Anne Lamott[6]

Recently in church we sang the hymn "Called as Partners in Christ's Service." It's a great hymn, and one that from the first verse not only convicts but also reminds what ministry in the church is all about. The hymn begins, "Called as partners in Christ's service, called to ministries of grace." It could just as easily be talking about raising kids, because if I have learned anything in the short time I have been a parent, it is that while there is a need for much work, raising kids is about grace.

Grace for Desmond and Anna—these little selfish, self-absorbed, but beautiful creatures that completely turned our world upside down. Not in the cheesy, sentimental way. In the hard way. Higher grocery bills—I am terrified of them becoming teenagers because we already go through a lot of milk and honey crisp apples. But, at the beginning, these little things couldn't do anything for themselves—eat, bathe, get dressed, or even wipe their own butts. They were, and still are, completely dependent on us. Desmond was a particular challenge because he was colicky. There were many nights when I had thoughts I am too ashamed to mention, and I am all the more thankful that grace prevailed for us.

Grace for Mihee—I was used to her being superwoman: doing everything, knowing everything, capable in almost anything. She had run marathons, written a book, hiked up mountains in her boots, and zipped down mountains on her snowboard. She was always up for a trip to the pub, a good restaurant, or anything random and fun. She could seemingly do it all. This was the woman I fell in love with many years ago.

During her pregnancy and now as a mom, I found that I often wanted the "old Mihee" back. The one who wouldn't forget everything or be too tired to do anything, and the one whose back didn't hurt all the time. The transition from "pregnancy brain" to "mom brain" wasn't easy for her, or for me. I wanted "Mihee brain" back. But that Mihee is not here, for now at least. And that is okay, because I needed to do a better job of embracing this new expression of Mihee.

It was all too easy to rely on her and to let her clean the cloth diapers, wash the onesies, get up in the middle of the night to comfort whichever baby was screaming, sterilize the bottles, and still have dinner ready for me when I got home from work. It finally dawned on me that I was not holding up my end of the partnership. My epiphany moment actually came while officiating a wedding at the church. Watching a young couple, who had hopes and dreams of their own, hold hands and publicly make their promises to love and care for one another, and basically be partners in their new life together, convicted me. It was then, as I began to do more and to offer Mihee more grace, that I realized that I had indeed fallen for the pre-baby Mihee, but I am still wildly in love with this Mihee. Her care, compassion, sacrifice, forgiveness, and willingness to be covered in snot, blood, vomit, yogurt, and applesauce reminds me of the One who came not to be served, but to serve. And I love her for it.

Reflecting back on that encounter with the other twin dad at the park has been good for me. Maybe that guy is right. Maybe we would be doing a disservice to the kids by not feeding them Rosetta Stone along with their scrambled eggs. But 100 percent of the time I will opt to raise these kids with that same love I experienced with my parents, and I will do it with my partner, Mihee, because with her we will certainly have many laughs, tears, joys, and, most of all, grace. As Desmond and Anna grow, love and grace might just be the best thing we can offer them. God knows we all need it.

Becoming Parents: More than Partners

While writings such as the Gospel of Thomas do show us a young Jesus, it is striking that the Bible is relatively silent when it comes to the lives of children and their parents. We do not get too many accounts of Noah changing diapers, or of Abraham and Sarah staying up way past their bedtime, even though they had a morning meeting, because they needed to rock Isaac to sleep and he just would not sleep some nights. We do not get to read about Moses having to arrange and provide childcare for the flock as he ascends the mount to receive the commandments. And in our canon we do not read much about the early days of Jesus. Sure, we get the birth narrative and the account of the flight to Egypt, just like we get a little bit of baby Moses in the basket. But besides issues of infertility and the continuation of the Abrahamic promise, we just do not get much in terms of having children in our holy book. Of course, we know that Jesus calls and welcomes the little children. We see that story on stained-glass windows almost every Sunday. But Jesus's welcoming call is a little different from parenting. While there likely are more, there is one instance of parenting in the Bible that, in my humble opinion, cuts to the heart of what it means to have kids, in the context of ministry or otherwise, pain and mistakes.

The account that comes quickly to mind is that of the boy Jesus in the temple. We all know the story. We are told he was twelve years old when his family made the trek to Jerusalem for the festival of the Passover. When it is all over, everyone packs up and heads for the exits on their way back home. Everyone, that is, except for Jesus. He stays behind, being a typical quasi-teenager and asking a lot of questions, perhaps questioning those in authority and showing them how much he knows. Finally, Mary and Joseph figure out that Jesus is not with them, so, in a panic, they head back to the last place they saw him, in the temple. And there he is with the teachers. I can only imagine their relief.

I don't know why Luke is the only gospel writer to give us this story and glimpse into the holy family. Perhaps the other writers did not want to embarrass Mary and Joseph for losing the Messiah. But I really think the beauty and the grace of this story being included in scripture is to partially remind us exhausted, hopeless, inexperienced parents that even the holy mother and father of Jesus screwed up from time to time. And somehow the boy still ended up all right. Mistakes are a part of the experience for every set of parents, even the holy ones. Even if they don't make their children learn four languages. Especially for Mihee and me.

While kids can potentially break our hearts and remind us of our own need for grace, they also bring us indescribable joy. I love that laughter played a role in the long-awaited birth of Isaac. It just makes so much sense. It might just be God's way of reminding us that while there is pain, sacrifice, and our patience is tested, if we are lucky, the birth pangs can lead to laughter and a joy otherwise unknown.

AFTERWORDS

> May all your expectations be frustrated. May all your plans be thwarted. May all of your desires be withered into nothingness. That you may experience the powerlessness and poverty of a child and sing and dance in the love of God the Father, the Son, and the Holy Spirit.
> —Blessing from Henri Nouwen's spiritual mentor[7]

Parenting is another one of those unpredictable pieces of life. It's completely different for everyone, and everyone has some kind of hardship. Whether someone is a single parent or in a blended family, whether extended family support is minutes away or in another hemisphere, whether the family has enough income to afford a nit nurse or not, there's simply no room to judge anyone. There are surely different things to negotiate—certainly some much more than others—but everyone has challenges. And there's no one way to do or be it.

This means that, however you and your partner work out, care for your children—that is it. You two know the best. It may not always work out smoothly. In fact, it probably hardly will because those little buggers—our sweet, angelic offspring—are somehow born experts at throwing wrenches into all our plans. But it's your life together. So whatever it looks like—whoever is the primary or secondary, whether the kids are with in-laws or at preschools, whether you do Ferber or Sears—what matters is that you do it together and you talk openly about it—constantly check in—and always, always leave a wide margin for error. The Bible and our theology doesn't say anything about what parenting philosophy

to use or even—contrary to popular belief—who should be the one always at home. That's where the Holy Spirit is vital. And this means
surrendering to the reality that we are not perfect. We are figuring it all
out together as we go along. It's not pretty most days. But it's still such a
gift.

—*MKK*

SUGGESTIONS

- Weekly house meetings to discuss finances, calendars, and the kids'
  ups and downs, as well as development and how we are going to parent
  them.
- One Sunday a month having the kids stay home from church to get a
  break from the constant pressure and attention. Even visit another
  church or worship service.
- If in the same congregation, embrace the opportunity to model being a
  normal family in church. Kids are loud. Kids need to sometimes be
  taken out of church kicking and screaming. Sometimes our kids
  wanted to sit up front with one of the parents pastoring that morning.

CONNECT

- What are your fears and expectations for being a parent and pastor?
- Who will provide the most direct care for children?
- How will you arrange it so that it fits your lifestyle and there is parity
  enough to provide balance for each spouse?

7

RE-CREATION
Valuing Sabbath Practices Together

MIHEE KIM-KORT

> Sabbath, in the first instance, is not about worship. It is about work stoppage. It is about withdrawal from the anxiety system of Pharaoh, the refusal to let one's life be defined by production and consumption and the endless pursuit of private well-being.
>
> —Walter Brueggemann [1]

The need for Sabbath is universal.

It doesn't discriminate based on race or religion, age or generation, species or gender. In Buddhism, the *Uposatha* has been observed since Gautama Buddha's time (500 BCE) and is still being kept today in Theravada Buddhist countries. It occurs every seven or eight days, in accordance with the four phases of the moon. Buddha taught that *Uposatha* is for "the cleansing of the defiled mind," resulting in inner calm and joy. On this day, disciples and monks intensify their practice, deepen their knowledge, and express communal commitment through millennia-old acts of lay-monastic reciprocity. [2] In a similar vein, in Christian culture Sabbath is lifted up almost as a requirement and obligation. In American culture, Sabbath is secularized and called a "day off," or "break," and might involve anything from going to church to playing golf to sleeping in to taking a day trip.

Lately, the topic of Sabbath seems a pressing issue with the numerous conversations taking place about the lack of it within and without the church. In particular, the exchange of ideas and thoughts about it on blogs, Twitter, Facebook, and books is certainly more apparent. One such book that is increasingly becoming popular (which I measure by how many times I see it come up on my Facebook wall or Twitter feed) is by Wayne Muller, called *Sabbath: Finding Rest, Renewal, and Delight in Our Busy Lives*. On the necessity for Sabbath for every human being, he writes:

> When we live without listening to the timing of things, when we live and work in twenty-four-hour shifts without rest—we are on war time, mobilized for battle. Yes, we are strong and capable people, we can work without stopping, faster and faster, electric lights making artificial day so the whole machine can labor without ceasing. But remember: No living thing lives like this. There are greater rhythms, seasons and hormonal cycles and sunsets and moonrises and great movements of seas and stars. We are part of the creation story, subject to all its laws and rhythms.[3]

This perspective on Sabbath emphasizes our creatureliness and the importance of seeing, knowing, and attending to this truth. Our creatureliness—that is, who we are as a creation and part of creation—is a huge part of what centers us in God.

It goes without saying that this is enough of a challenge in our current day and age. Add being married to it. Add being a pastor to it. And then add being a parent to it. And then add being married to a pastor to it. Perhaps *challenge* is a bit of an understatement.

Sabbath: Full Work Days

> The most valuable thing we can do for the psyche, occasionally, is to let it rest, wander, live in the changing light of a room, not try to be or do anything whatever.
>
> —May Sarton[4]

I love church.

Growing up, Sundays were full. We would get up early in the morning, usually hauling containers of food or packages of paper towels to the car to donate to the church. The thirty-minute drive was a little sleepy, but as soon as we stepped foot through the church doors and saw other families, we stirred and started immediately to run and play. Other parents would yell at us to "slow down," or tell us to *insa*—respectfully greet the adults who were elders and deacons of the church—or try to slap us on the ass (really, only one elder would do this to us—by today's standards he was a bit of a creep, but was seen as the crazy uncle of the church), which would make us squeal and scream and run away even more. Worship for the adults would begin upstairs, and we would run downstairs for our own lessons, and then finish early to play and sneak bites of the lunch that was set up. After lunch and cleanup, when we were older, there were youth group Bible studies and gatherings at people's homes, and then finally, maybe close to dinner, we would be home, and my dad would mow the grass while Mom cooked dinner and we did our homework.

I loved it all. It was almost like a holiday or family reunion every week.

When Andy and I shared our church experiences with each other, I was often surprised how much he spoke with indifference. Church was not as big a deal to him growing up. I suspect it had something to do with being a PK (pastor's or preacher's kid) and the fact that he did not rely solely on the church as his main community. He had friends from school. Friends from sports teams. Friends from his neighborhood. However, even though I had friends in school and on my street, the community at church felt the most familiar. Perhaps it had something to do with seeing my parents feel more at home, too. They seemed more comfortable, and more at ease.

Technically, it wasn't really a day off. Certainly not for my parents, who got up just as early, sweated and worked just as hard, and went to bed just as late that day as any other day. And we were busy in Sunday school and youth group and choir or practicing for various holiday programs. But it didn't *feel* like work, so did it count?

Looking back now, it seems our little church truly embodied the Acts 2 church.

> So those who welcomed his message were baptized, and that day about three thousand persons were added. They devoted themselves to the apostles' teaching and fellowship, to the breaking of bread and the prayers. Awe came upon everyone, because many wonders and signs

were being done by the apostles. All who believed were together and had all things in common; they would sell their possessions and goods and distribute the proceeds to all, as any had need. *Day by day, as they spent much time together in the temple, they broke bread at home and ate their food with glad and generous hearts, praising God and having the goodwill of all the people.*[5]

There's work here. They are distributing necessary items to those in need. But there's meals. There's praise. There's connection. When we went home from church at the end of the day, we were tired. But it was a good kind of tired, a purposeful kind of tired, we felt full. Full of hope and perspective. We felt ready, centered, and focused for the week. We would make it through another week. We would make it.

Sabbath: No Days Off

After becoming a pastor, and being married to a pastor, Sundays felt full in a different way. And not quite in the way that was like my childhood. It was still church, but the way I experienced it was markedly distinct. When Sundays overflowed with departures from the house in the dark, to-do lists, and running from one program to the next with every minute seemingly scheduled, it felt less like church to me and more like Monday–Friday work. When both Andy and I got home, we were utterly exhausted and unable to do anything. Lunch was barely a meal at home, and usually it involved scrounging on snacks and leftovers or having food delivered to us. We would immediately get into our pajamas; he would collapse on the long couch, and I would fold myself up into the large sofa chair. In the appropriate season, we would turn on the football or baseball game and fall asleep to the sounds of announcer commentary, crowd roars, and whistles.

During this time, Andy's "day off" was on Friday. My "day off" was on Thursday, which may seem random but fit well for me, since all my energy was poured into youth group on Wednesday nights. I put quotation marks around it because, of course, something always seemed to come up, whether pastoral visitations or emergencies or funerals or work from the week that did not get done and bled into our time away. So we had days off. Sort of. We had church on Sundays. Sort of. And Sabbath? We had snatches of Sabbath here and there with a trip into NYC or getting away to read a non-work book over coffee. The first year of living in our first home we were in walking distance of a pub/bar. We spent many a Thursday and Friday night reliving our seminary days sitting and drinking most of the night away. It was fun, but it was actually never really restful.

Looking back now, if I were to define the quality of my life based on the amount of Sabbath I engaged in on a regular basis, I would say that it makes sense I was so stressed out all the time. *It was because our Sabbath times were undefined—they were haphazard and largely unintentional. In essence, they were neglected.*

To flourish requires some kind of fracture in the day-to-day routine, temporary but thorough and extreme. But a large part of me believed that a genuinely faithful Sabbath was about *doing nothing.* I perceived that this further meant not scheduling, not planning, and not even thinking about anything, even Sabbath. I thought it was about vegging out or sleep. I personally needed to crash for a few hours, and I really needed to be alone (i.e., away from people and obligations, including Andy). During the winter of my first year at my second call, I started to go up to a nearby ski mountain in the Poconos to snowboard alone all day. And this was the first time in a long time since seminary, since field education, since ordained ministry, that I felt I was truly experiencing some kind of Sabbath. Barbara Brown Taylor speaks of this in terms of faith and lifestyle, which is also relevant here:

> To make bread or love, to dig in the earth, to feed an animal or cook for a stranger—these activities require no extensive commentary, no lucid theology. All they require is someone willing to bend, reach, chop, stir. Most of these tasks are so full of pleasure that there is no need to complicate things by calling them holy. And yet these are the same activities that change lives, sometimes all at once and sometimes more slowly, the way dripping water changes stone. In a world where faith is often construed as a way of thinking, bodily practices remind the willing that faith is a way of life. [6]

Carving out space for pleasure was restful, whether it was carving up a whole roasted chicken for dinner or carving out lines in snow. Part of re-creating Sabbath required reframing it in terms of enjoyment, literally, to take joy in the simple and ordinary gifts of every day, and making space to attend to these activities. Sleep is great, but even it isn't always as restful and restorative as doing more intentional and nourishing activities that have to do with one's interests.

Sabbath: More than Nothing

However, I could see Andy being depleted by the lack of Sabbath he continuously had as a solo pastor, since almost everything at church fell on him.

My original assumptions about Sabbath were off. Sabbath was not exactly about doing nothing. And as a married person, Sabbath was not always about doing nothing. Andy and I were starting to deviate from each other in work in terms of our ministry passions and styles, and we were also veering away from one another in our rest. *And we realized it was not only in our work that we found the necessary commonality and overlap, but also in Sabbath rest that we were truly able to experience a more important connection again.* We needed time, space, and rest to connect to each other in a meaningful way.

A friend recently blogged about an article by Jonathan Safran Foer in the *New York Times*, called "How Not to Be Alone," that challenged me. When I experience stress, I have a tendency to retreat into technology and myself. But this is not how I wanted to live this season, and I certainly did not want to form a habit that would make me always live this way.

> Psychologists who study empathy and compassion are finding that unlike our almost instantaneous responses to physical pain, it takes time for the brain to comprehend the psychological and moral dimensions of a situation. The more distracted we become, and the more emphasis we place on speed at the expense of depth, the less likely and able we are to care. Everyone wants his parent's, or friend's, or partner's undivided attention—even if many of us, especially children, are getting used to far less. Simone Weil wrote, "Attention is the rarest and purest form of generosity." By this definition, our relationships to the world, and to one another, and to ourselves, are becoming increasingly miserly. [7]

This translated into *not* thinking about taking care of everything at work. No smartphones (which is still a huge challenge for me). No emails. No Facebook or Twitter. No texts. *Sabbath, for us as a couple, would mean taking care of each other.* But sometimes this would even mean leaving each other alone as long as there was mutual agreement. Sometimes, this would mean deliberately scheduling a time, even if it meant a few hours on a work day, to be together. Just us, maybe food or coffee, and a place where we could simply be in the community. In Easton, we loved mornings after the big rush at the Cosmic Cup coffee shop, where Andy became good friends with the owner, Troy. We would eat bagels (not always the best tasting) and drink coffee (always great) and chat for a while, read newspapers, or sit and read together. Granted, this meant we would inevitably run into church members, but while that might have felt like "work," it was a good reminder that we were not just public figures but also people who lived in the neighborhood like everyone else.

Like a path through the forest, Sabbath creates a marker for ourselves so, if we are lost, we can find our way back to our center.

—Wayne Muller[8]

It was a good way to remember we needed time off just like everyone else. No distractions. No commitments. No work. To pay attention to ourselves. To pay attention to each other. To pay attention.

ANDY KORT

Schedules: Days Off and Rest

> When Jesus had crossed again in the boat to the other side, a great crowd gathered around him.
>
> —Mark 5:21

After I graduated from college, I worked in retail for a short time. As anyone who has ever worked in this industry knows, the work schedule can be all over the place. On the plus side, I usually did not have to clock in until 10 a.m., a not-too-early morning for someone who still liked to bar hop. On the down side, my schedule had many late evenings and, even worse, weekends.

Most of my other friends I was living with then had what seemed at the time like "real" or "professional" jobs. They wore a tie to work and were home by 6:00 p.m. (or later if they went to happy hour). They also had every weekend off. Holidays, too. The hardest part about working on the weekends was knowing that I was missing out on the fun my buddies were having together. Lounging by the pool, golfing, sleeping in, or eating wings and watching college football were among the many things that I felt I missed out on as I was at work stocking shelves, scanning merchandise, and trying to answer the customer's questions.

Instead, I would have a random day off, like a Tuesday. Tuesdays off are great if you need to run errands or are an introvert who likes alone time. In some respects, it was not bad. I actually did enjoy my job and my co-workers, but I began to long for the elusive weekend with two days off in a row. Eventually, I would leave retail and take a "real" job, where I, too, had to wear a tie and had weekends off. Ironically, I missed the retail schedule. I came to see that places are more crowded and some things, like golf, are more expensive on the weekends. At the time, I had no idea how my experience with the retail schedule would prepare me for the unpredictable and intrusive schedule of a pastor.

After graduation from seminary and upon starting my first call, I was faced with the option of being able to pick my day off. My head of staff had Mondays off, although he never took them. Realizing the potential for two days off in a row, like many other clergy, I quickly pounced on Fridays as my day off. It was the same thing at my second call. As a solo pastor, I could pick any day I wanted, and, once again, I took Friday.

Growing up and watching my father as a pastor, I saw how necessary it was to not bring work home. Even though he might not bring sermons or books home all the time, I could see that his mind was still at the office. When the phone rang at home, it was usually for him because there was some kind of pastoral need. I started to hate hearing the phone ring during dinner because I knew that it would take him away for the evening. And yet, in my ministry, my day off was soon bombarded with extra work that prevented me from truly being off. So I started to feel that I needed to at least complete the physical separation. No books. No emails. No physical reminders of the work.

Sometimes this meant hiding out in my room in my pajamas and sleeping a little more. But this did not help me rest as much as I thought it would, whether I slept in or took a snooze in the afternoon. Sometimes the physical separation required driving twenty minutes away to another small town to find a coffee place where I could be completely anonymous with no worries but making sure I had enough gas to get back home. A change of scenery. A spot to be completely anonymous. Sometimes Mihee would tag along, and even if we said very little to each other, it was a chance to breathe and be together.

The point was to find a time and place to rest.

Schedules: Interruptions to the Routine

> Every person needs to take one day away. A day in which one consciously separates the past from the future. Jobs, family, employers, and friends can exist one day without any one of us, and if our egos permit us to confess, they could exist eternally in our absence. Each person deserves a day away in which no problems are confronted, no solutions searched for. Each of us needs to withdraw from the cares which will not withdraw from us.
>
> —Maya Angelou[9]

I have come to greatly appreciate the passages in scripture that describe Jesus and his attempt to get away, be alone, take a break, and refresh after a grueling bit of ministry. There is a great sense of permission given in there for pastors who struggle with the idea of taking a day off. If Jesus sought out downtime, then by all means so should we in our own lives. Of course, if we keep reading, we see that Jesus seemingly rarely gets his desired break or time off. The crowds keep coming.

As a solo pastor, I learned sooner than I would have liked that solo really does mean solo. A solo pastor is often alone with little or no other staff support. Like the unpredictable retail schedule of my days gone by, I experienced the call to clock in at times that were not always best or convenient for me. Hospitalizations, illness, surgeries, deaths, and other emergencies do not take my schedule and calendar into consideration. And that is fine. Part of the calling of ministry that I consider a great honor is being able to be with people in their times of need and in crisis.

Of course, these also occur on Fridays. And when they do, part (and sometimes all) of your day off is gone.

Then there are the times when there are no emergencies, but works still creeps into the day set aside for rest and rejuvenation. The copier goes down, there is a staff issue, someone needs pastoral counseling, a member stops by the office not wanting to take up all of our time but stays forty-five minutes, and evening meetings need advance preparation and planning. If you are serving, or have served, a church, I do not need to tell you how easily forty hours a week becomes a lot more. And the crowds keep coming. Is the work really ever done?

One could easily say that since I am in charge of my own schedule I should, and perhaps could, set some clearer lines and boundaries. And I do that at times. Working during the week away from the office or having the secretary hold my calls are two ways I have done this. But, thanks to the information age we live in, I still get emails, texts, and phone calls that can quickly change all of those good intentions. The crowds keep coming.

A friend and colleague of mine in ministry recently shared with me a story that illustrates this point. He described how he would often go to a public park in Pittsburgh for some rest and time of Sabbath. While he was there, he noticed the high volume of pigeons, doves, and other birds in the area. One day, he decided that he would bring some bread to feed the hungry pigeons. So he brought with him four loaves of bread, only one loaf shy of what Jesus had to work with as five thousand hungry souls waited to be fed. My friend unwrapped one loaf, and then another, and another, and another. But it wasn't enough. He said, "I really thought that four loaves of bread would be enough to feed the pigeons in the park. But they just kept coming and coming and coming. I didn't have enough to go around." Ministry often feels like that. There is not enough of us to go around as the crowds keep coming.

Remember the Sabbath day, and keep it holy.

—Exodus 20:8

RE-CREATION

105

Many times ministers do not get much help for those around us. Have you ever noticed that ministers are held to a lower standard when it comes to the Ten Commandments? What I mean by this is many times we are only expected to keep nine of the ten. If we keep all ten, then we might be viewed as aloof or lazy. One of the great mysteries and paradoxes of the life of a minister is the notion of Sabbath. Many times pastors are encouraged, or in some cases expected, to break the fourth commandment. Among other things, Exodus 20 instructs us to "Remember the Sabbath day and keep it holy." Yet Sunday is the busiest and most exhausting day of the week for pastors. And it is not just because of worship. We often have meetings right after church ends or we have to run to the hospital or we have to keep our ties on because we need to get back to church for the committee meeting that night. It is exhausting. The crowds just keep on coming.

Recently, this happened during a particularly busy Christmas season. In addition to the normal Sunday commitments, we had two or three extra worship services in Advent. During that Advent and into early January, we also had four funerals and one wedding. I never got to experience or enjoy Christmas that season. Truth be told, Christmas was a major burden that year rather than the enjoyable experience I assumed everyone else was having during Christmas. I felt terrible for Mihee not only because she had to put up with my grumpiness but also because I was not around to celebrate the season.

But the reality is that the crowds keep coming. And the gospel writers tell us that Jesus keeps ministering to them. His time, the disciples' time, and (as clergy) our time is not like everyone else's. I have finally come to see that Sabbath has nothing to do with comparisons to other people's lives and schedules. After all, another commandment deals with coveting those things.

Schedules: Making Space

Ultimately, I have come to realize that a day off is not necessarily a Sabbath. And a Sabbath is not necessarily about a day off. I say this because, on our days off, Mihee and I end up doing all of the other stuff we were not able to get done during the week because of work and because of the kids. Things like going to the grocery store, mowing the lawn, or sitting down to pay the bills. And we'd go to bed just as tired as we would during a normal work day, even on Sundays. I do not think the point of the fourth commandment is for us to do nothing or to simply have fun. While it may be those things, I think at the heart of the commandment is to whittle out—even imperfectly—time and space for us to step away from work, schedules, agendas, and our lawnmowers, and to instead step toward God and God's Word.

I recently have reread Dietrich Bonhoeffer's *Life Together*. It is fascinating to see the parts I underlined more than ten years ago while in seminary. I still am drawn to most of those highlights, but I underline different lines now. For instance, in his chapter "The Day Alone," he points out that our meditations on scripture are not only for the understanding of a whole community but also for us individually to see what is "God's Word for me personally" on a given day. I think he's right. Maybe a true Sabbath is a time and a place where one can hear what God is saying to them on a given day at a given moment. I don't think God's voice to us is limited to Sundays, or whatever happens to be our day off. Sabbath nuggets throughout the days of the week are often enough, like a good powernap, to see us through another day, another week.

To help us with this, in the spirit of St. Benedict and St. Gregory the Great, Mihee and I have instituted our own "rules." The point of the rule, and we both made different ones, is to help us in what we call "holy living." They include things like running, cooking for each other, taking turns watching the kids (mostly for Mihee's benefit), and stepping away from technology for two hours a day. But the rules also include spending time reading God's Word, not for work or for sermon preparation, but rather for our own edification (I'm currently reading through the gospels). I am also reading through my denomination's *Book of Confessions*, albeit slowly. We do much of it separately, but some is done together. And we hold each other accountable for doing it. The rules contain elements of rest, rejuvenation, and worship. In its own way, it allows for a little Sabbath every day, which we need because Sunday, the Sabbath day, is a work day.

It is enough to remind us that we need God and God's word to sustain us, to empower us, to encourage us, to instruct us, to remind us that God is God and we are mere creatures. A day of Sabbath is about our own rest, yes, but it is also about God, the worship of God, which hopefully inspires us toward works of justice, mercy, and compassion. And then maybe there might just be enough of us to go around for at least one more week, even as the crowds keep coming.

AFTERWORDS

I can barely come up with a business that is actually closed on Sundays. Chick-fil-A—the popular fast-food chain that originated in the South and professes roots in Christian principles (and recently was in the media limelight for controversial statements about homosexuality)—is the only one that comes immediately to mind. Not doing business on a Sunday is so counter-cultural it is shocking. I myself have driven there on a Sunday after church craving waffle fries only to be dismayed—and mostly annoyed—at their CLOSED sign. *Who is closed on Sunday?!?!?* A prime business day??? Of course, in a society that values excessive work, and competition compounds the pressure to achieve, produce, evaluate, and "climb the corporate ladder," the church also stands as an odd fixture. Any amount of free time should be filled with "getting things done," like cleaning out the gutters, catching up on work, or running errands, right? *Sitting in a pew??? For a whole hour and fifteen minutes? That's an utter waste of time! We need to get to things; after all, time is money!*

Perhaps pastors, too, struggle with this concept of taking time off. Whether due to the pastor's workaholic tendencies or the inability to get away from work because of the lack of support staff, it is one of the bigger challenges in our vocation. When family obligations get mixed into it (whether immediate or extended—I am thinking of elder care or caring for one's disabled siblings, and not only children, as a couple of examples), the lines between work and home get blurred because all of it is equally taxing and requires mental, emotional, and physical energy. Eventually, it feels like there is never any time off, and certainly never a chance to really catch a breath.

A valuable mentor often shared with me that Sabbath is basically "catching one's breath." And the meaning goes deeper. If our breath is to our bodies like the breath of God is to the body of Christ, then there's something significant there for our lives. In a way, our breath also contains our spirit. When the Holy Spirit is missing from the body of Christ, then there is nothing to hold the community together. Likewise, if we don't take the occasion of catching our breath, we lose ourselves to our work, our families, our obligations, and everything else, and who we are begins to fall apart at the seams. This applies to our most important relationships (and not only marital) and cultivating that necessary time and space is essential to our survival.

—*MKK*

SUGGESTIONS

- Take time to write down concrete activities or non-activities each person needs to catch one's breath. Make a point to schedule them in whether on the family calendar or Google calendar.
- Have someone take care of the children in their home on a Saturday, so you can have a morning or afternoon (or both) at home without any other responsibilities. Less bodies in the shared space makes a big difference.
- Go into your room or office at home, close the door, and lock it. Don't come out for an agreed-upon amount of time.
- Look at the five-day work week as fifteen blocks of time; make sure each partner has at least one block of time off, and that there is one block taken together.
- Realize that "time off" will look differently in every season, and that you need to adjust accordingly.
- Schedule a babysitter for one night of the week for two hours for dinner and house meeting.

CONNECT

- How do you catch your breath?
- What is the biggest obstacle to your ability to Sabbath?

8

CHURCH ON SUNDAYS

Pulpits and Pews

MIHEE KIM-KORT

> The vocation of pastor(s) has been replaced by the strategies of religious entrepreneurs with business plans. . . . The pastoral vocation in America is embarrassingly banal. It is banal because it is pursued under the canons of job efficiency and career management. It is banal because it is reduced to the dimensions of a job description. It is banal because it is an idol—a call from God exchanged for an offer by the devil for work that can be measured and manipulated at the convenience of the worker. Holiness is not banal. Holiness is blazing.
>
> —Eugene H. Peterson[1]

Sunday church.

This was the pinnacle of our work week. While the mornings seemed solely full of kids running off to Sunday School or adults gathering around the carafes of coffee before classes, meetings, or forums, it was the few minutes before worship that garnered the most excitement and energy. No matter how exhausted we were as we slipped into the black robes, there was an undeniable buzz, and it was contagious.

Church became a challenge as we saw what was missing from our own worship lives that was different from the families of our churches, or our seminary friends where one spouse was the pastor of the church and the rest of the family worshiped there. The old adage "you can't have it all" applied to so many seasons of our lives, and this was no exception. We both felt called to full-time ministry. We both felt called to family. We both felt called to worship together.

It wasn't meant to be so simple to work out. But this was a time to reframe the experience and space of church, both within our actual churches and then, after we had children, within our homes. It was a time of creativity and invention, where we could be and do church in a variety of ways while being faithful to our roots. We would tentatively start to find small ways to plant seeds of faith in the children, and find those seeds taking root in us as well as we gave the language and songs of our faith tradition to them.

We would experience church in a myriad of surprising ways.

From the Pulpit: Seeing Families

As a solo pastor, Andy preached weekly. This was mind-boggling to me. While I enjoyed this part of ministry, I would flail and flounder, and get frustrated with it. Thrash and almost tantrum about the process, and the end result. When my turn would come up, which was about once a month (sometimes twice if my head of staff went out of town), I would think with all good intention that I would start working on it three weeks prior. Then two weeks prior. All of a sudden, it was Friday night before the Sunday I would preach, and I would panic. I would bombard him with questions:

> "Where are all my commentaries on the Psalms?!?!"
> "Did you take them, Andy?!?!"
> "Give me a story to use about the demon-possessed pigs!!!"
> "Do you have a joke or introduction?!?!"

For obvious reasons, he learned to avoid me when I was in my full-throttle sermon-writing mode, and when it got closer to Sunday.

Some might see this as procrastination. I prefer to call it a warped sense of perfectionism. Even during the children's sermon on Sunday mornings, I would still be making slight changes and edits to the sermon, though it was done more out of uncertainty, and an expression of nervousness. Like being a fidgety preschooler, it was akin to tapping my fingers or twiddling my thumbs. When the organ music would fade quietly as parents returned to the sanctuary from dropping off children in the nursery or childcare room, I could feel my heart quicken a few hard and fast beats. My mouth would dry up, and I coughed to clear my throat. But as soon as I began the usual prayer, I felt weirdly blanketed by an unexplainable calm.

Lord, may the words of our mouths and the meditations of our hearts be pleasing to you, our Rock and our Redeemer.[2]

I would launch forward and sail.

Regardless of whether the sermon was "good" or "successful," I always enjoyed the preaching. *It was not simply the act of preaching— talking or teaching or presenting or so forth—it was the act of seeing.* It was sharing. It was living. It was feeling. It was being. I loved relating to the congregation. Of course, there were at least a dozen heads nodding off to sleep. That was fine. I don't mind helping people get a little rest, especially if they have children. It's a way of Sabbath. I understand now that this might have been the only chance. But perhaps my eyes would catch someone's eyes as they sat there in the pews. When I would feel something deep and true about what I was saying in the moment, and felt it reverberate across the sanctuary, resonating in some way, I felt it on my skin. It was more than affirmation. It was a reminder of how words, and the Word, through the movement of the Holy Spirit, mysteriously but tangibly forges those undeniable connections.

There was also something about seeing the look between family members. A knowing, loving look between a mother and daughter, a father and daughter, between siblings. An unexpected smile or laugh. An acknowledgment and expression of understanding. Those connections between family were precious, and likely rare with the way family's schedules were crammed with so many appointments, games, shows, practices, and so on. I loved it but it made my heart ache a little. I wanted to be in worship with Andy on Sundays. And when we would eventually, and hopefully, have children, I wanted them to be in worship with their daddy and mommy, too.

And then we became parents.

One Sunday morning, I woke up late with the twins after another long night of nursing, and disaster was waiting for us in the living room. I walked right into it. It's rare when both babies are crying and clinging at the same time, but, on this particular morning, it was the norm. Neither would be consoled, and every toy was a reason for battle. I barely chugged my one cup of coffee to become a little more alert. But I wanted nothing more than to duck for cover and find shelter in my bed. Sunday church? No chance. I stopped for a moment and stared at my options. The door. My car. The bathroom. I really needed to go to the bathroom.

I looked at my iPhone and jumped on Pandora, picking the church music station—not exactly contemporary music, but not organ either. A rousing rendition of "Come Thou Fount of Every Blessing" with piano and mandolin came on, and the babies quieted down. Other songs came on with a little more energy, and so I picked them up and danced around the room with them while singing the hymns at the top of my lungs in an operatic voice. They squealed and threw their heads back. When they seemed to quiet down, I found an old sermon of Andy's dad's and played it. While I listened, they were content to mouth the stacking cups, and then bang them together for emphasis like little amens. Afterward, we had a few crackers, a little mushed-up baby food, and milk. By then they were ready for a nap.

I took a deep breath. Looking around at the mess of toddler chew toys and dirty spoons, I reflected, "Was this church?" We sang hymns. I said numerous prayers (albeit alone and mostly quiet, many confessional) and even more petitions. We listened to the Word proclaimed from a recording of a sermon by their grandfather, Pap Kort. We shared in an ordinary meal, and although there were no words of institution, and I only had a few crackers and a little apple juice, my eyes were opened in a way I imagined was similar to those disciples who encountered Jesus on Emmaus road.

In the Pews: Being a Family

When we both became pastors, we struggled for a long time with the thought, "We now do not have any days off." Little did we know that we were actually in paradise and living it up before the kids, because there is no day off when you become a parent. And so Sunday needed a major overhaul. Moving to a town where Andy would be the head pastor of a church and I would be stay-at-home meant that home was where we needed to be the most, and no one was going to find any semblance of rest at home. I grappled with the loss of so much in that first year of the twins' lives: job, church, community, and, most of all, a Sunday routine we had just figured out together. At some points, it felt like I was losing an emotional, spiritual, and physical battle.

But we both hunkered down. In the new town, Andy left before dawn on Sundays, and I stayed with the twins, woke them up, fed them, dressed them, and coaxed them into the car. As they got older, it was easy to bribe them: "We are going to go see Daddy! Yay!!" Sometimes I was more excited than them. When they were small, though, there were Sundays that were impossible. The night before might have been full of numerous wakings, or one of them might have been up because of sickness or teeth. These were the days the struggle was constantly close to the surface, and always breaking in, so Andy and I would snip at each other, sometimes fighting over the most absurd minutiae of the day. Eventually, I would realize that it was the angst I was feeling in this time of transition and sacrifice. Although I joked often that my new church was tiny and had two members, our twins, I felt demoted and demoralized most days. I missed being a minister of a church.

I eventually found solace in our pew.

Like many diehard Presbyterians, we found our own pew. We didn't mean to have one. In fact, before having the kids, I mildly railed against those who claimed a pew, especially those cringe-worthy stories of people who would even kick out the unknowing visitors innocently sitting there. I never understood it. But we just kept finding ourselves in the same pew, mostly for the sake of convenience. It had proximity to the doors that led to a small chapel for quick diaper changes, stairs to the nursery room, and a speedy exit out of the church. It is not in the front, and it is not way far back. And there is a large space between our pew and the next section of pews in front of us. It allows the children to roam a little, if necessary. So I bristle ever so slightly when I see anyone sitting there now, before I realize that there is an opportunity to connect right in front of me.

Sitting in the pews as a more permanent fixture, and conscientious of being on display for better or worse, I saw just how much worship was transformed for me by the mere presence of our children. I thought about all the young families that showed up to my previous churches and felt in awe. *How in the world did they do it?* It is no easy task. Despite the reassurance that many people would step in to help at the drop of a hat we were obviously solely responsible for these children. *So my eyes were always open by necessity, and this changed not only the way I prayed but also how I was present.* Because my eyes were occupied with the where-abouts of the twins, I relied on my ears. Music became much more meaningful, and I caught much more during the sermon. The many textures of worship—passing the peace and passing the visitor book, receiving the light streaming in through stained glass windows and watching young acolytes carry the light in and out of the sanctuary, rising and sitting in rhythm with the liturgy—it felt brimming over with possible meaning.

Sunday church is anything but banal and boring. What our children have done for us is provide another dimension, not only to our vocations as pastors but also to our experiences of worship and faith. There is something holy about the mess and chaos of children, and when it is even a part of the polished and impeccable space that is typical Presbyterian worship, it gives us a different meaning to God-with-us and the kingdom-among-us in worship. But I would be lying if I didn't say how much I relished the gift of peace and quiet when the children could be in the nursery. To have a moment where I didn't have to battle or fight against anything but could soak up the holy in that place and time was priceless.

ANDY KORT

> You will never cease to be the most amazed person on earth at what God has done for you on the inside.
>
> —Oswald Chambers[3]

As a preacher's kid, I never fully worshiped with my family. We were all in the same worship space, the sanctuary, but I was with my mom and my sister, while my dad was far away, up front, with only his profile visible. With Mihee serving at her churches following her ordination, it was the same thing. I was not worshiping with family. This time, the person I was closest to was not even in the same building. It was not ideal, but a necessary vocational hazard of being in a clergy couple. I think we got used to it, but there was a persistent nagging feeling that something was missing in our lack of ability to share something so important, the worship of God, with the person closest to us. Although we relished the occasional opportunity to lead worship together, it was extremely rare that we would ever worship side by side.

Yet, as a clergy couple, we do not have the luxury of worshiping together in the traditional way because, well, Sunday is a work day. And Sunday morning has the most visible and pressure-filled work hours of the week. But if Sunday is a work day, especially Sunday mornings, how in the world can a minister worship? *Snow White's dwarfs tell us to whistle while we work, but can we also worship while we work?* It has taken me a while to get here, but I believe the answer is a resounding yes.

But it has not been an easy road. Often it still is awfully treacherous trying to navigate this dynamic. The move from pew to pulpit is drastic. The view literally changes from simply following along in the bulletin to thinking about what is next in the bulletin, where we will stand, what we will say, how we will say it, and worrying that the minute for mission will actually go on for fifteen minutes. We go from staring at the back of people's heads to seeing their faces. If we are Presbyterian, we go from sitting as far back in the sanctuary as possible to sitting up front. We go from easily lifting our eyes to see the cross hanging above the chancel to having unobstructed views of the exits and the sound board in the back. Yet it is this changed view that allows me to worship God on Sunday morning, even while I am "on the clock."

Those who set up a fictitious worship, merely worship and adore their own delirious fancies; indeed, they would never dare so to trifle with God, had they not previously fashioned him after their own childish conceits.

—John Calvin[4]

I have learned that worship really is more than an hour on Sundays. Planning and writing liturgy is a faithful act of worship. Crafting a sermon is an act of worship. There is a lot of administration involved in preparing for worship, but there are a lot of opportunities for small worship-filled moments packed with confession, a call to faithful discipleship, prayer, the need for grace, and the longing for good news. So my experience of worship has shifted a bit. But it still very much involves Sunday mornings. And now it is mostly because of the view.

I often wonder if the faithful in the pews realize how much we can see as we sit up front. This terrifies me as I think back to some of the things I did while seated in the pews. When I was younger, I would occasionally sneak in the small pocket-sized television I got for Christmas one year. Trying to hide the antenna, I'd search for reception of any kind. (I am glad smartphones did not exist in the 1980s and 1990s.) I would also write jokes back and forth with my friends on the back of the bulletin. I even fell asleep from time to time. When I was in high school, my friends and I would occasionally sit in the front row and try to make the preacher (my dad) laugh. He never did laugh at any of our antics.

Some of that still goes on in the pews. People continue to talk to their friends during the sermons, people still try to hide using small electronic devices, people still do not pay attention, and people still fall asleep. I can see it all. Some of it bothers me, and some of it does not. But the vast majority of people there on Sundays fully worship God. And it is all beautiful.

On any given Sunday, as I am seated up front in my black robe, and after I make sure my wireless microphone is turned on, I pause to prepare for worship. Then I open my eyes and I see the children of God gathered, and sometimes still coming in, to worship God in the sanctuary.

I see husbands and wives sitting together. Some hold hands and others do not.

I see newlyweds and couples celebrating sixty-two years of marriage.

I see single moms, and I see mothers there by themselves because the husband does not come with them. I see young parents with small children. I now know the struggle it takes to get those kids here, and I am moved by their presence. Often, the daughter will climb into her father's lap, while the mother helps the son follow in the bulletin by pointing to where we are and what comes next.

I see older siblings helping a younger one find a hymn in the hymnal and awkwardly hold the increasingly heavy blue songbook out so both can sing.

I see an older woman sitting with other older women who have also lost their husbands. They are a family of sorts now.

I see a widower sitting by himself. He is in the same pew where he used to sit for decades with his now-deceased wife. It is impossibly hard, but he still comes to worship.

I see newcomers whose story I do not know, but I can see they are in worship here and now for some reason.

I see a man in a tie, and I know he is pulled in a million different directions at work. I see his wife and know that she has much on her heart and mind, including the health of her mother several states away.

I see an elderly woman, a matriarch in the church, sitting with a walker, and I see another saint of the church help her steady herself as she stands to sing a hymn.

I see kids squirming and drawing in the bulletins, ready to spring forward down the center aisle for the children's sermon up front.

I see teenagers looking completely bored one minute and sitting on the edge of their pew hanging on every word of the gospel the next.

I see someone who has just returned from surgery with a look of relief on his face.

I see someone who will be moving soon to take a new job out of state, a little uncertainty etched into his face.

I see men and women dressed in white robes sitting behind me—a preview of the heavenly choir, perhaps.

I see the tears, and I see the smiles. I see the grumpy faces, and I see the laughter. And I see so much more. All of them, the children of God, there with all their pain, hurt, grief, sadness, worry, stress, burdens, joy, gladness, hope, faith, and longing. Sure, some are there as a part of their routine, but I believe all are there for a glimpse of the God who loves them. And for an hour at least we are there, all of us, to worship God. And the Prelude on the organ continues.

The service I have designed is now in motion. Liturgy and prayers are said. Hymns are sung. Scripture is read and proclaimed, and hearts and spirit are hopefully nourished by it all. And, I can only hope and pray, the Spirit works through me to help them worship God. *But the great secret they do not know is that they help me worship God in ways they cannot begin to understand, because in my view from the front I see the story of our faith in all its living and incarnational beauty.* I still worry about where to stand and prepare for what is next, but I do so surrounded by the saints. In the midst of that great cloud, the Spirit can move even the most preoccupied preacher to worship God in all God's wondrous glory.

We are to be lights in the world. It is God's business to light us, to set us on the lampstand, and to bring the people into the house. Our only duty is to shine forth with the gospel.

—Marva J. Dawn [5]

Of course, I look out and see Mihee and the kids. Her mere presence reminds me of the honor I have to be a pastor to these people. I am reminded of the sacrifice she made for me, for us, so that we could be in our current situation. I know it is hard for her in ways that are beyond my comprehension. Because, if the roles were reversed, I am not sure I could do the same thing. But she is there. And she has the kids climbing all over her, or she's chasing after our oldest son, or she's singing with our daughter who is standing on the pew, or she's feeding our newest little blessing and providing him a liquid and milky form of manna that I am unable to give him. Many times, she will hand off one of the twins or the new baby to someone around her. She may be thinking of it as a moment of rest or a break. I see it as the baptismal promises in action. I see it as her trusting a member of this community to care for this child, if only for a few moments, just as they promised to do at our children's baptisms. I see her remain seated in the pew for a hymn because someone has fallen asleep on her lap. Other times, I see her stand to sing in her beautiful voice that belongs in our choir. I see her offer me a nod of encouragement after each and every sermon while she mouths, "Good job."

I see her there in her familiar pew, knowing she longs to be up front, and I am reminded of the grace, the love, the exhaustion, and the sustaining support in her faithful oblation to me and to God. I may be the one in the black robe sitting up front, but the Spirit moves in mysterious ways, and by all of this she preaches to me. Week after week she, and others, preach to me from the pew. I look out at Mihee and see the gospel proclaimed not with words as much as by actions. And let me tell you, she can really preach it!

I have been to the Grand Canyon and stood atop Pike's Peak and the Empire State Building. I have seen the Pacific, the cliffs of Ireland, and the impossibly blue waters of the Caribbean. However, I am convinced this weekly Sunday morning view is the best of them all. I offer a prayer of thanksgiving for her, the kids, the community of faith, and the presence of God in our midst. Our family is all together as a part of the full family of faith. And I worship God in gratitude and praise.

AFTERWORDS

> That is what worship is all about. It is the glad shout of praise that
> arises to God the creator and God the rescuer from the creation that
> recognizes its maker, the creation that acknowledges the triumph of
> Jesus the Lamb. That is the worship that is going on in heaven, in
> God's dimension, all the time. The question we ought to be asking is
> how best we might join in.
>
> —N. T. Wright[6]

Sunday church is a whole other animal for a pastor's family, and even
more so now, as we have recently discovered as a clergy couple's family.
Whatever the job situation for both partners, Sundays are never straightforward and easy. There are days we have to juggle two churches, if I'm
providing pulpit supply for another church, while Andy does his normal
worship leadership and preaching at his church. Coordinating childcare,
pick up and drop off, and their time in the nursery and in the sanctuary
with a family—it isn't exactly child's play. Some Sundays, we would
have to leave the children at home with a sitter because the running
around wasn't working out or even worth it. At the same time, I couldn't
help but feel deeply guilty that the children were missing church.

Church is not just a vocational obligation for us as pastors—it's a
necessity. Granted, there are days I would rather go without it, and push
the snooze button a dozen more times. But, with children in our lives, it
feels like being among the gathering of believers is all the more urgent.
The sanctuary is a sanctuary for our family, even if there are times we
feel like we are being watched and scrutinized, or even people's amuse-
ment and entertainment. It reminds me of God's constant presence, God's
being as a refuge and comfort, and God's love and grace after a week of
being beat down and tested in a myriad of ways. And it is a time of
healing and help, but I can't imagine anything else that we would want to
impress on our children during that holy hour. Being among God's beloved creation worshiping God is what should be the core of who we are
as individuals and as a family.

—*MKK*

CONNECT

- What do you need or expect to experience on Sunday mornings? Are there family traditions or routines that nourish you?
- What is your Sunday situation, and what are the logistics you have to plan in order to have a meaningful day?
- What does it look like for you and your family to worship together?

9

COMMUNITY

Encouraging Friendships and Connection

ANDY KORT

> Friendship is born at that moment when one person says to another:
> "What! You too? I thought that no one but myself . . ."
>
> —C. S. Lewis[1]

"**H**allelujah!"

This single word is the typical start to every conversation with Jay, one of my closest friends in ministry. We met my second year in seminary, the same year I met Mihee. We are both from North Carolina, and we were next-door neighbors in our seminary dorm. Jay and I now live in different states, we are in different roles in our church, and we serve in different denominations. Yet he, and others, sustain me in my ministry.

The word *hallelujah* is a Hebrew word roughly translated to mean "Praise the Lord." Why do Jay and I begin every conversation with that word? Jay and I have been talking on the phone almost every weekday for several years now. I think saying "Hallelujah!" started as something of a joke. Or perhaps it was something sarcastic, like "Hallelujah! You finally answered your cell phone!" Yet, over the years, it has evolved into its right meaning. It is a shout of praise to the Lord for the opportunity and the gift of connection with a dear brother in the faith who just so happens to be a great friend. Plus, he's funny as hell. Someone who can make me laugh so hard I have to use my inhaler is definitely a keeper.

Connect: Picking Up the Phone

> It is more fun to talk with someone who doesn't use long, difficult
> words but rather short, easy words like "What about lunch?"
>
> —A. A. Milne[2]

Many times our conversations are short. I would guess they last five to seven minutes. We typically call each other as we are in our cars driving to work. It is one of the few free and alone times either of us will have all day. Not only is Jay in ministry, but he also is married with two small children. For the two of us, the drive into work (and home again) is often the only real time of being alone all day, and, for me at least, there is a sanctuary feeling to the inside of my car. Amid the crumbs, candy wrappings, dust, dirt, receipts collected with pennies in the cup holder, I find a quiet sanctuary from the noise of both work and home. That is when I am not listening to the Counting Crows, Pearl Jam, or NPR. These short conversations are only as long as either of our commutes, depending on traffic. Once we pull into the church parking lot, it is time to hang up and head inside for the day and the work at hand.

Of course, we often miss each other and have to leave messages, although Jay admittedly hardly ever checks his voicemail box. But when we do connect on these short calls, it is wonderful. Sometimes we only talk about basketball or some random current event. Other times we will talk about what Jay had for breakfast or what coffee shop I'm headed to for the morning. Much of it is mundane and somewhat nonsensical. But even in those conversations, there are real connections. We always share what our schedules are going to hopefully be like that day. We talk about any important meetings that day, or we will process a meeting from the night before. We talk about church dynamics and the myriad of interpersonal relationships that are most mentally demanding. Sometimes, especially if Jay is preaching on Sunday, we talk about the text and share ideas. Other times we vent about life at home or at the church. And then one of us pulls into the parking lot, and we say another "Hallelujah!" while preparing to hang up, knowing that one of us will likely call the other some point later in the day. But I also know that there is someone I love and trust who is aware of what I have going on that day. Jay prays for me, as I do for him, and it is a gift to know that he's at least thinking about my ministry, my life, and me as I begin my day. I find this life-giving in the midst of the loneliness of ministry.

Comfort: Finding a Third Space

I am sure that I do not need to go into great detail regarding the loneliness of ministry. Despite being around people all day long, there are many times we are in the office completely alone. My car is the only one in the parking lot. I spend a lot of time in my car alone, at the church alone, and walking by myself around town alone. I do value that alone time, but it is far too easy for a sense of isolation to creep in if we do not have anyone with whom to share ideas. It is hard to vent, process, and reflect on much of ministry alone without going a little crazy talking to yourself all day long.

There is also the delicate balance of being "friends" with members of your church while still maintaining an appropriate distance and professional boundary. Also, I don't know too many pastors who would be willing to spill their guts to a parishioner. I know I don't feel this is completely appropriate. But those guts need to be spilled somewhere. If you have a spouse, that can work at times. If your spouse is in ministry, that can work, and he or she will likely understand most of your situations. However, I am aware enough to know that I already dump enough onto Mihee with the kids and all my other insanity. So I need another space, a safe space, a third space. I need friends like Jay.

The majority of my conversations with Jay are short. But at least once or twice a week one of us will really need the other, and we stay on the phone, sometimes for close to an hour. So we sit in our cars in the parking lot, or we shut the doors to our offices, and we talk. But this time it is not about biscuits, coffee, the latest *Sports Illustrated*, or anything else like that. We talk about what is going on in our lives and in our ministries. The hard stuff. And we are open. We are vulnerable. We are honest with each other. We talk about calls and sense of call. Jay helped me process and think through our recent move to Indiana. We talk about a conflict, an issue at the church, or a struggle or an imminent challenge on the horizon. We dissect and analyze hard meetings in greater detail. We also talk about fights with our wives. We talk about frustration with our kids. We share challenges and the stressful burdens in our family lives. Jay was the one person I told about our infertility issues. I vividly remember sitting in the church parking lot in tears, telling him I did not think Mihee and I would ever become parents. We also challenge each other, push the other to dig deeper, hold the other accountable, and call out the other person's

"BS" in a supportive way. But, most of all, we are a safe space for the other in a vocation where there often is not an abundance of safe spaces. And this is crucial because one of biggest challenges for ministers is the sense of being and feeling alone, even if you are in a clergy couple.

Mihee gives me the gift of having this time and space with Jay. Often the phone will ring with his unique ring-tone, so we all know it is Jay calling. And she knows I need the space to process and talk through things that, frankly, she doesn't have the energy or desire to think or talk about with me. Plus, she knows that Jay and I laugh a lot, and that I need that space to be an idiot, too.

Circle: It Takes a Village

> When we honestly ask ourselves which person in our lives mean the most to us, we often find that it is those who, instead of giving advice, solutions, or cures, have chosen rather to share our pain and touch our wounds with a warm and tender hand. The friend who can be silent with us in a moment of despair or confusion, who can stay with us in an hour of grief and bereavement, who can tolerate not knowing, not curing, not healing and face with us the reality of our powerlessness, that is a friend who cares.
>
> —Henri J. M. Nouwen[3]

In my friendship and conversations with Jay, I have learned that we all need people to support us. We all know that. We teach that, we preach that, we counsel that. But pastors, at least many that I know, do not seem to be good at having people who support us. Or honestly hold us accountable. I have been blessed on several occasions by Jay challenging my assumptions and calling my logic into question. He also gave me a much-needed attitude adjustment when I would get frustrated with another Saturday funeral or holiday interruption. In one of the churches I have served, I had stretches when I seemingly had funeral after funeral after funeral. So many that I began to complain about it constantly. The icing on the cake was a pastoral emergency on Thanksgiving Day. Instead of watching the Macy's Thanksgiving Day parade, I felt like I was watching the Death Parade complete with an enormous Grim Reaper balloon flying overheard, and I was the grand marshal.

I picked up the phone and instantly began griping to Jay about how all I wanted was to have a relaxed holiday with family like everyone else, only to see that go up on smoke. He said, "Andy, that is what pastors do—it's the job. Yeah, it sucks, all these funerals are right in the middle of your Saturdays and that happened on Thanksgiving. But that family needs you, and you are their pastor. So take some extra time off during the week to make up for it."

And he's right. I needed to hear that straightforward reminder. It cut through my grumpy tantrum. That's what a good friend does for us—they honestly and genuinely hold us accountable. Maybe I've matured, maybe I have made peace with Saturday funerals and holiday interruptions, or maybe I have simply realized that these are some of the vocational hazards for pastors. But that's OK because being a pastor is an awesome privilege, honor, and joy. And somehow I've seen how these things kind of balance themselves out. Jay helps me see all these things and more. I know that I need someone to do that for me—someone that isn't always Mihee. The outside set of eyes and perspective is able to see, hear, and understand things in ways that Mihee and I cannot, since we are sometimes "too close" to the situation. There are times when Jay is likely able to be more honest with me, and less concerned with having to live with me and my hurt feelings than Mihee might be, in the midst of juggling the emotions of all our lives.

I am much better at this practice of staying connected than Mihee. I don't know why, but she's terrible about picking up the phone and calling a friend. She's aware of it. I have tried to encourage her to make more phone calls and face-to-face visits. On two or three occasions, I have arranged for a friend of hers to fly in to see and surprise her. I always love watching her in those moments. But instead of picking up the phone, she chooses to stay connected online via Facebook, Twitter, and other platforms. It used to drive me crazy, and honestly it still does a little, to see her constantly staring at a phone, iPad, or computer screen. But I have begrudgingly learned this is how she stays connected to her friends, so I am trying to be better at giving her that space. She also needs these connections, even if she's connected in a different way.

In PC (USA)'s *Book of Common Worship*, there is an element in the wedding liturgy that I absolutely love. It is called "Affirmation of the Congregation." Essentially, it is a moment in the ceremony when the friends of the bride and groom stand and promise to support these two in their life together. During that time, these friends are no longer mere spectators enjoying a wedding while looking forward to the wine at the reception. They are now actively engaged in this couple's life together as they, too, stand and promise to be present in this new journey. As the bride and groom gaze out upon the congregation, I am always struck by the power of that moment. It is as if part of the great cloud of witnesses suddenly materializes and becomes visible. I think I am always moved by this moment because I know how much we all need friends to uphold us, support us, care for us, and keep us honest.

No doubt ministry is hard. Lonely. Stressful. But the support of a good friend is powerful. *A good friend is the presence of Jesus Christ in a moment that is bleak or hopeless.* I remember in that moment that Jesus told his disciples that they are no longer servants, but friends.

Hallelujah!

MIHEE KIM-KORT

> Our lack of community is intensely painful. A TV talk show is not community. A couple of hours in a church pew each Sabbath is not community. A multinational corporation is neither a human nor a community, and in the sweatshops, defiled agribusiness fields, genetic mutation labs, ecological dead zones, the inhumanity is showing. Without genuine spiritual community, life becomes a struggle so lonely and grim that even Hillary Clinton has admitted "it takes a village."
>
> —David James Duncan[4]

There's another voicemail.

I know who it is already. I watch the phone flash with the name "Andy Kort" and a tiny picture of him with the twins. I'm in the middle of cooking or changing a diaper or driving or coffee with someone, and I think, "I'll just call him back."

He hates it when I do this to him. He knows I am sitting there watching the phone ring with his name on the screen. And he knows—and, I guess, I also know—that I will likely not call him back. He especially hates when I do this to anyone—friends, family, coworkers. We will be sitting in the room, and my phone is next to me, clearly ringing/vibrating/flashing, and I just glance at it. Andy looks purposefully at me.

"Aren't you going to get it?" he asks.

"No."

"Why not?"

I shrug. "I'll just call them back when I'm ready."

"What if it's something important?" He starts to get annoyed.

"It's OK."

"Just answer it!" he exclaims.

"Nah." I'm barely audible as I wave his exasperation away.

I can't help it. Except for three people in my life, I almost loathe talking on the phone. I love being with people—a solid ENFP on the Myers-Briggs—but for the life of me I can hardly muster up energy to talk to people on the phone. Face-to-face? Fine. Text? Fine. Voice-to-voice? It requires total and complete mental energy for me to dive into the conversation. The surrounding situation has to be just so for me to feel present. Likewise, I have to feel awake and comfortable, and maybe need a chance to brush my teeth or lather on some chapstick. And find my earphones.

Why is it such a big deal? I'm not sure. There is something about phone communication that has always been a struggle for me. I'm painfully aware of how awkward I am—with no physical cues, I often interrupt the other person, or I mumble and talk too fast, so I feel like I'm constantly repeating myself. I hate repeating myself. And I start to do something else—it feels wrong to just be sitting there and be so . . . *unproductive*. So I avoid the phone. And now, with the technology we have that allows for us to be connected in other ways, like through Twitter and Facebook, not to mention email and text and Voxer (although I haven't really gotten into that last one), I feel it's not necessary to always be on the phone. There are other ways to find meaningful connection.

Virtual Community: More than Status Updates

One of the aspects of social media many people—and not just Andy—bemoan is the onslaught of mundane information. This is mostly why Andy decided to get off the grid. He didn't feel it was necessary to see another picture of someone's expensive steak dinner or to see a conversation between a married couple expressing their undying love to each other or whether someone liked *someone else's* status or photo. It was simply too much to be updated all the time. Or to know what people were thinking all the time. And to constantly turn down invitations to play Farmville or Candy Crush.

And while I'm inclined to agree with him about the nuisance of too much information, I am dependent on these little moments of overlap with others. These others include family, friends both near and far, and friends whom I have never met IRL (in real life). I get to see what they see a little—whether they are travelling or simply going to their office. I get to see their children—both human and furry—and how they are growing up all too quickly. I get to vent and curse in private Facebook groups with people who are completely supportive, even though we've never met each other and probably would never know each other without the opportunity to be in this little tribe together.

Something about it echoes the Acts 2 community to me: "So those who welcomed his message were baptized, and that day about three thousand persons were added. They devoted themselves to the apostles' teaching and fellowship, to the breaking of bread and the prayers" (Acts 2:41–42).

This devotion—the regular and passionate commitment—to gather together and learn the Way and care for each other is practiced in the virtual world. I know most people would argue that this continuous self-reporting and self-regulation is narcissistic. It's terribly obnoxious. But we share stories through blogs. We provide links to articles. We Google Hangout, and sometimes there's food. We pray for each other and with each other. I have one Facebook friend who always posts lyrics of a favorite Gospel or hymn and then a Bible verse first thing in the morning. Some days it's a little aggravating, depending on my mood, but for the most part I love it. It's consistent. It's genuinely joyful. It's encouraging. And it's exactly who she is as a friend and minister. Even these little pieces of her are enough to get me going for the day.

Still, I know that this isn't enough to sustain a person or community *all* the time. We need to be with each other in the flesh-and-blood.

Physical Community: Beyond Hashtag and Twitter-Speak

Since having children, I discovered it's strangely easier—as they become more mobile and uncontrollable—to stay home. I've never been much of a homebody. I want to go out. I want to be around people; I want to breathe fresh air and see more than the walls that feel like they're caving in on me. I want to remember what it's like to be a human being among other human beings.

Perhaps, I'm being a little melodramatic. I'm not on house arrest, but sometimes it feels like the children are laying siege to my sanity when we are holed up. I'd rather deal with that battle because the other option is a major production—to put on their SSJ (socks, shoes, and jackets) is a fight to the death. But lately my saving grace is playdates. There's another human adult and someone else to help me "parent" my children for two hours. And I can finally go to the bathroom uninterrupted and unhurried.

More than that, I can have an actual conversation. I'm not limited to 140 characters. I can verbally process without feeling like I need to sound witty or even interesting. I even don't have to use hashtags.

#lifeasarealhumanbeing #whataconcept

There's a whole other language in the blogosphere and Twitterverse and in this odd world that sits backlit on our tablets and smartphones. If I had the time and energy to do some theological and cultural analysis that would be relevant to these topics, I would do it. But for now, it is enough to acknowledge that while that world opens up so many possibilities for learning and language, culture and community, *it's not meant to replace human touch.* Even Skype and Facetime, and whatever other video communication, is missing the shoulder to cry on or the touch of a person's fingers on your hand—even the meaningful eye contact. We were meant to be face-to-face, to have our breath mingle with another and veritably inhale the smell of another person. It may sound odd. Scents and odors are almost more embarrassing than anything else, and we often don't describe a person in terms of smell unless it's truly offensive. I wonder if it is because of the level of intimacy associated with it. But that's exactly it. Life on the screen prevents genuine intimacy and connection from occurring between two people. I'm not talking about sexual intimacy— certainly that occurs, whether it be through pornography or sexting, but even that isn't truly an intimacy in the sense of the presence of authentic personhood. The intimacy God meant for us is messy, smelly, and awkward, but also where we are able to see each other fully.

When Andy and I lived apart, it was difficult to maintain the depth of connection necessary for a young marriage. Physical proximity is a basic human need. Likewise, when I am alone most of the day, even though I have the children, I need to be around other people. The moms' group I have found myself in is largely the random result of missing the cutoff for one new moms' gathering and going to another group, where the twins were older by two–three months, and then getting together at the library or park on a regular basis. We've forged bonds simply by coming together in our exhaustion, desperation, and angst. But there's joy, too, when we share the mile markers of watching the babies learn to crawl, then walk, then run and babble conversations. These women have become my anchor to sanity and survival these first two years, and what a blessing—the care they have shown me throughout this time of adjustment, and then the surprise of baby number three. Andy sees what I need for the day-to-day, and even though it is different and almost foreign to him, he gives me space—time, quiet, and a strong Wi-Fi signal.

Still, "virtual" might be a misnomer. *What happens in my communities online is just as real as the bread I break with the people next door or at church on Sunday mornings.* There are just too many ways to feed and be fed by others, and throughout all the various seasons, my friends float in and out of my days, like travelling companions struggling with the exact same demons or guardian angels holding me from afar. And it's all so good and important. Marriage, ministry, and mission—all these have changed my understanding of the church, family, and friendship. They've stretched and broadened what friendship looks like on a day-to-day basis, and the long-term commitment. In the days of my childhood when friendship was based on simple things like sharing a class and maybe living on the same street, I experienced it narrowly like a one way street. But as I've grown up I have seen how friendships ebb and flow, and the ones that are rooted in empathy and generosity always have lasting power. The friendships that continue to bless me the most are the ones where I can pick up the phone after a three month silence, even a year-long silence, and we can easily begin again where we last left off.

Throughout it all, my sense of family and community continues to develop and widen to include those that are not related genetically or biologically. The mingling of tears is a strong adhesive. And this can happen in person—and across oceans.

AFTERWORDS

> The glory of friendship is not the outstretched hand, not the kindly smile, nor the joy of companionship; it is the spiritual inspiration that comes to one when you discover that someone else believes in you and is willing to trust you with a friendship.
>
> —Ralph Waldo Emerson[5]

Andy and I do friendship differently. I wouldn't chalk it up to stereotypical gender differences, although it certainly does apply sometimes when I hear Andy talking sports or movies. When I finally met some of Andy's friends from college, I couldn't help but laugh at some of the frat-boy clichés and all their antics. Truth be told, they were kind of obnoxious together, but also kind of endearing and charming. I could see right away that there were special connections, and so much of who Andy is today is because of these friendships. Though they don't keep in touch nearly the same as before, there is something so paramount about all these relation- ships that touch our lives whether positive or negative.

Since time is truly a scarce commodity, we know we have to make space for those relationships that truly sustain us—and, of course, it's usually a two-way street—so this means that the amount that Andy receives is proportionate to how much he often gives to the friendships. This also means that sacrifices are sometimes made—time away from the family whether for a few minutes in a separate room or out to a coffee shop—so that those conversations can happen in an edifying and worthwhile way. Whether or not community happens over the phone or in real life, we have learned that the time away from each other is well spent when it is with people who genuinely sustain us by walking with us.

—MKK

CONNECT

- Where and how are you fed by community? As individuals? As a couple?
- How do you provide yourself with space to find restoration through others?
- Do you need gentle reminders to stay rooted in your support community, and, if so, in what way?

10

CALLING

Faithful Discernment and Response to God's Grace

MIHEE KIM-KORT

> We have to recognize that there cannot be relationships unless there is
> commitment, unless there is loyalty, unless there is love, patience,
> persistence.
>
> —Cornel West [1]

Andy and I met in the summer of 2001.

At the time, I was actually dating someone else. A lot of mileage was
put on my Subaru because of this new infatuation I had with this boy who
lived in Denver. Shortly after our first meeting, we started dating. I was
elated. But when I received my acceptance to seminary, his friends
started to ask me what we would do, and whether we would try long
distance. They were worried about my commitment. They were skeptical.

I assured them, and him, that we would do the long distance, and it
would work out fine. We even started to talk about how he could look up
programs nearby, sell his share of the house, and move near me so we
could eventually be together. And I really believed it could work. At
least, I tried to make myself believe it—after all, he started to make plans.
And so I made plans, too.

But then Andy came into my life. And, like a typhoon, he burst
through my plans, shattering any and all thoughts of the future.

Granted, it wasn't immediate. Andy and I became friends, and then good friends, and then 9/11 happened when I was on a surprise trip back to Colorado to visit family and friends. As airports closed, indefinitely cancelling all flights, I didn't have a way back to the East Coast. But Andy was in the Midwest somewhere with a friend, so he suggested I find a way to get at least halfway. My father rented a one-way car for me to drive to Kansas. Andy drove from Ohio to Kansas, and I caught a ride back to Princeton with him and two other students. When Andy drove his familiar Honda Passport into the parking lot where we arranged to meet in the middle of Kansas City to drop off the rental, my heart stopped. He stepped out. I ran into his arms. It felt like I had come home.

At this point, we still weren't really "official." Even so, I knew then that this was it. He would show me what grace looks like in all its disastrous and impossible glory. He would be the one to incarnate a different kind of faithfulness. He would be my home. We would walk in this life together, and I would learn about community, ministry, and family in new ways.

Giving Thanks: Sharing More than the Holidays

> Rejoice always, pray without ceasing, give thanks in all circumstances;
> for this is the will of God in Christ Jesus for you.
> —1 Thessalonians 5:6–18

One of the biggest challenges in marriage is to negotiate time with the in-laws. Usually the time is centered around the holidays, particularly Thanksgiving and Christmas. The holidays may provide some sweet sentimentality but they are most likely full of stress and high expectations. They are fraught with difficult-to-navigate dynamics, especially in those first years of marriage. Based on the advice of other couples, we tried to give equal time to both families each year and alternate holidays. Some years this would work out well, except the very nature of our work caused everyone to drown in a lethal cocktail of high expectations and high-energy activities, which resulted in, well, some holiday grinchiness. Honestly, we spent a lot of time asleep and hardly any time really sharing in the holidays. But really, despite all the little family squabbling, it was always good to be home.

Since Christmas felt like one long marathon because of Advent programs, the new favorite holiday became Thanksgiving. With only a lovely meal as a requirement and little possibility of commercialistic frenzy encroaching on this holiday (although now businesses are open on Thanksgiving—as if Black Friday wasn't depressing enough), it had felt much more like a holiday we could truly celebrate together. No programs. No activities. No extra worship services or sermons. Except when we were in Easton. We thought it would be a nice idea to create opportunities in which we would work together in worship. We would lead worship together. And Thanksgiving Eve was an evening when some churches actually held a worship service, so we collaborated and did a joint service between our churches alternating locations each year. Our intentions were good, but then it took away another week when we could simply rest and be together during a holiday.

One year it felt like everything was catching up to us. We were to lead the Thanksgiving Eve service at Andy's church, and I was slated to preach the sermon. The week before and, for some reason, on the day of the service, I felt harried and rushed. Advent was a program-heavy season for me, with activities for children and youth right away in December. Everything from buying ribbon to practically living at Michael's, to going through too many gluesticks, to clipping a bush in the churchyard (for greens for the Advent wreaths—apparently I was the only one who did anything to trim that shrub) avalanched what little time I had to prepare for this worship service.

When we arrived at church, we tried to get situated in his office. I carried my robe in and threw it on a chair. He looked at me.

"Here. Give me your robe."

Andy picked it up and hung it on a hanger smoothing it out for me.

"Was this balled up in your car since Sunday?" He didn't wait for the answer he already knew was coming when I simply shrugged and said, "Yeah."

He shook his head and sat down at his desk. I milled around looking for candy and found a container of Skittles. Thinking it would help assuage my nervous energy, I started to pop handfuls into my mouth. A little stale, but still sweet. He looked up at me again, and asked, "What. Are. You. Doing?!"

"Nothing. I'm hungry. I didn't have time to grab anything, and I need to wake up a little. Leave me alone!"

He went back to looking through his bulletin and highlighting various parts while I ogled the books on his shelves.

"Hey! Isn't that my book?" I exclaimed pointing to a Bonhoeffer book.

"No. It isn't." He didn't even look up when he replied. "Do you need a highlighter to go over your parts of the service? Do you have your scripture passage ready? Your sermon together?"

"I'm fine." I waved my hand at him. "Don't worry, I got it."

He shook his head again. "Okaaaayyy," he said. It sounded more like "You don't look like you've got it, but whatever."

Since I was also singing in the choir, I left him for a few minutes and went to rehearse with them. When it was almost time for the service, I walked back and donned my robe. He was ready to go and waiting for me. We started to walk out, and I realized I'd forgotten my sermon. I ran to get it. We went out into the hallway, and I realized my lips were dry, so I ran back to get my chapstick out of my coat pocket. The door was locked. Exasperated, Andy dug out his keys and unlocked it. I grabbed the stick and slathered it on and stuck it in my pocket. As we walked out again, he asked, "Are you sure you have everything?" I looked around. "I think so. Yes. I do. I think."

Surprisingly, it was smooth sailing when we processed in with the choir and went through most of the service. I felt present and engaged in the delivery of my sermon, and that little tingling that comes with really feeling the passion of the words. Usually that happens when I am utterly exhausted and give myself over to the moment.

And then we were getting ready to do communion. There was a large display of pumpkins and squashes in front of the communion table with some dried ears of corn—a beautiful harvest presentation. But it was a bit crowded. Somehow we were supposed to walk down and around the table and then back up behind it in between serving the elements. Without knowing it, my mic had fallen off my lapel and was dragging along the sanctuary floor. I tried to squeeze by the communion table again, and we heard a loud crackling over the sound system. I looked down and saw my mic wire tangled up in the dried ears of corn. My eyes widened. The only way to get it out was to keep walking. I put my hands over my ears, like most of the congregation.

Oops.

Andy was already standing behind the communion table just watching me. And, of course, laughing at me. I frowned at him, and then turned my face to the organist—who was also smiling—so the congregation wouldn't see me, and mouthed, "Dammit!!" but guffawed silently.

What a mess.

I couldn't help but feel . . . overwhelmingly silly. And young. Immature. Embarrassed. Almost as if I was play-acting up there or playing dress up and pretending to be a professional clergy. And I realized that the struggle with identity and authority, confidence and competence, never completely dissipates. Granted, this was during my third year in ordained ministry, and such a long time ago now, but I realize now that in different ways I need to see that my vocation and calling would not come from Andy or look like Andy's, much less anyone else, and I would need to clasp for dear life the promise of God's good creation, which includes me—with gratitude.

Of course, all this happens with the one I call home—Andy—and in that refuge and space I live freely and courageously into who I am.

Giving Thanks: Faith-Full Living for All Our Days

> One of the tragedies of our life is that we keep forgetting who we are.
> —Henri J. M. Nouwen[2]

Perhaps it isn't coincidence that I write this near Thanksgiving, Advent, and Christmas. Being thankful, joyful, hopeful, peaceful—all of it starts to blur together when I try to figure out the fundamental goals of my faith. I wonder if it is simply that—faithful living. And living faithfully means living in the here and now, living in the present, and always living with thanksgiving for all the pieces of one's history and the promises of the future. So it seems they, in a way, go hand-in-hand, faithfulness and gratitude, which is why I'm drawn to gratitude as the word that characterizes my ministry, my identity, and my call. Not that I am good at being grateful—quite the opposite—but it is crucial for how I intentionally live as wholly God's. It is a *posture* for all of life.

This kind of posture not only allows but also encourages a creative flexibility. Call is not limited to a formal kind of ministry—validated by a community or governing body and accompanied by benefits and pension; it is instead, I've discovered in my own life, a response of gratitude that is

an offering of the best of who I am for the sake of God's kingdom. In this
latest season, since I stopped working full-time as an ordained minister to
be at home with the children, I have found—and been found by—a number of ways to live out the passion and gifts cultivated in me by God's
gentle spirit. They range from serving on boards, including the Presbyterian Mission Agency, where I chaired one of the committees, and the
community and editorial boards of the Young Clergy Women Project, to
starting a campus ministry at Indiana University. It is truly difficult to put
a price on sane, adult conversation with other adults concerning topics
beyond whose turn it is to pick the TV show. Truly, something I took for
granted up until now.

Sometimes these ministry opportunities are small projects here and
there, whether event planning for churches, blogging and web design, and
then writing projects. All the little things I could squeeze in between
those brief moments the children didn't absolutely need me were possibilities for ministry—cleaning out the fridge or shoveling dirt at the
nursery school or simply taking a meal over to a family from the church
or community. It didn't matter—I jumped on it. Those Sundays I filled
the pulpit for another church in town were nourishing opportunities for
my own soul—feeling the pulpit beneath my hands and sinking comfortably into my familiar black robe.

And it helps me to see the necessity of faithful discernment within my
call. And our call. I remember one of the first conversations about parenting I had with close friends from seminary, John and Noelle, during my
pregnancy with the twins, and they said something that stuck with me:
"Parenting is continuous discernment." I loved this little nugget, but the
weight of it made me sink into my chair a little. I'm terrible at making
decisions for myself some times, and definitely for Andy. We often spend
more time trying to decide who will make the decision than actually
making the decision. Yet here I was reminded that the need for deciding
was inevitable, so it made sense that it would translate not only for the
way I would care for my children but also for my call. For our call. For
our family now.

The combination of marriage and the vocation of ministry is a strange
soil for growing in God. Nevertheless, a successful harvest is not ensured
by the existence of that soil. *Rather, it is the thoughtful and measured
cultivation of faithful discernment—choosing—together, and not simply
choosing situations or wallpaper or a kind of car, but choosing each*

other through it all. Everything else is ultimately pointless unless we are choosing each other and our life together as the result of our marriage and the fruit of our ministry. And for all the imperfections, all the seemingly terrible decisions we have made together, all the hardships, I am experiencing a kind of liberation in my vocation despite what is going on in our lives and who is working at what church. Or not working at a church.

As we continue to grow together in grateful and faithful living—both vocationally and in our family life—I can't help but see the ways God's grace is present and real in my life, and long to respond passionately no matter what the venue or season.

ANDY KORT

> If we commit ourselves to one person for life, this is not, as many people think, a rejection of freedom; rather, it demands the courage to move into all the risks of freedom, and the risk of love which is permanent; into that love which is not possession but participation.
>
> —Madeleine L'Engle[3]

> We have to keep asking ourselves: "What does it all mean? What is God trying to tell us? How are we called to live in the midst of all this?" Without such questions our lives become numb and flat.
>
> —Henri J. M. Nouwen[4]

"Tell us about your sense of call." This question in one form or another is, without fail, always asked during interviews by Pastoral Nominating Committees, higher governing bodies, and others when talking with a potential candidate for a ministry position. At least, it has always been asked of me. While I am sure they are interested in my "sense of call," I sometimes wonder if they really want to hear why I am interested in whatever position and how I think my gifts might fit. Of course, they ask me that question about my gifts, too. But it is interesting to me that once we get past that initial question and the years of ministry together march on, we are never, or very rarely, asked about our sense of call again—that is, until we happen to interview with another committee in another town.

Recall: Reflecting on Call and Gifts

I believe a big part of our job in ministry is to help others, usually the laity, understand and discern their sense of call and then to help them live into it. We equip them, we train them, we empower them, we listen to them as they tell us "I want to help the church, but I don't know what to do," and we try our best to help them figure it out. The point is to expand and to share ministry in the church, so that each saint of God can embrace his or her own gifts. For some it is making sure coffee hour happens every Sunday, or reading liturgy in worship, or crunching numbers for the budget, or making sure the church's roof isn't leaking into the sanctuary, or organizing mission projects. The list is endless and the acts of helping others discern their call—it is also ceaseless. And that's a good thing.

This is not limited to individual members. We also help communities of faith discern their calling in ministry in a certain time and place. But, in my experience at least, ministers are rarely ever asked about their sense of call while they are serving a church. We are not even really encouraged to talk out loud with members about it. I cannot help but wonder if that is because there is an underlying fear that we may say something that makes it seem we want to leave them or are feeling called away from them. If we are being honest, the reality is deep down they know, and we know, that it is extremely rare for someone to stay in one church, one nonprofit, one seminary position, or one job for their entire career. But maybe they don't ask because they assume we will stay there forever.

However, another reality is that we are often "re-called." To be sure, that means we can be called again and away from our current situation. But that also means we can be re-called, or called again, to our current situation as God continues both to do a new thing and to bring to completion the good work began in us. As most people already know, the hard part continues to be discerning God's ongoing call. In other words, it is hard to figure it out. Maybe it is good they don't ask us, because we might not always know.

Much has changed since my first call. I am married, I have three kids, I became a homeowner, I am older, and, in some ways, I am wiser. My perspectives and priorities have also changed—there was no choice. My call, and Mihee's call, now affects three other people. I have learned much from my experiences in both life and ministry. One of the greatest lessons I have learned along the way is simply this: our plans do not often align with God's. I know that you know this already. But what I mean by that is I think we often try to control our sense of call and the call process. By doing so, we are trying to control God. That won't work.

I believe God honors our gifts, skill, and desires. Therefore, I can rest easy in my assumption that God will not call me to be a music director or organist. That being said, I am not convinced that we can dictate to God where we will or will not serve, when we will and will not serve, and how we will or will not serve the kingdom. Until we moved to Indiana, I really wanted to live within an hour of New York City, and preferably closer. Why? Because I love the city. I love the Northeast. It is fun and exciting, and there is no place (in my mind) like it. My discernment went some-thing like this: "OK, God. I am ready to listen to your soft, still voice. Here I am, Lord. I will go Lord, if you lead me. As long as it is within an hour of New York City. You see God, I love New York and Yankees games and Knicks games and the subway and the museums and Central Park and that place in Chinatown where I can get really good pho. And while we're at it, I'd really like to go to a church that is downtown somewhere, so I can walk to coffee shops and restaurants and be sur-rounded by nice people. Oh yeah, if you can, God, please make it a church with money, so I won't have to stress about the budget or the building falling apart. Like I said, here I am Lord, send me."

Relinquish: Limiting God and Letting God

I was trying to control God. I know this is a familiar struggle to many of us. I was trying to limit what God could do with me, only giving God a small area of the world to work with. I've learned that doesn't work. I have learned that the ministry at a place, not the place of ministry, is important. Some of my friends have also learned this. When they discern new calls, they begin by telling me all about the city, town, state, and so forth with great excitement long before they ever tell me about the church itself. When they do talk about those things, it is usually along the lines of "Well, you know. It's ministry. I'll be doing the usual stuff." And they always end up leaving those calls after a short time. I cannot, and should not, speak about their experiences, but I am reminded about our tendency to want to control the process and God.

But I do not think I would be faithful if I was not continually discern-ing my sense of call. Are my gifts and skills still a good fit for my current place of ministry? Do we share a similar vision and understanding of mission after five years together? Is the way I lead worship consistent with the way they prefer to worship God? Am I spiritually feeding them and are they feeding me? Is this still a healthy community for my family? On a good day when things all go right, the answer to those questions is likely "Yes, I like it here, and I'd like to stay here." Then there are those days we all know all too well, like on a bad day, or especially during a bad stretch of days, we may be thinking, "God, please get me out of here."

I relate to the Rev. Adam Smallbone, the vicar at the fictional St. Savior of the Marshes in London on the television show *Rev*. In one particular episode, Rev. Smallbone is dejected and struggling with the idea of serving the people in his community. We get the sense that he would rather be doing anything else if it were possible. When a colleague asks him about the esprit de corps in his office, Rev. Smallbone rolls his eyes and sarcastically answers, "Love the vocation. Love the people."

In that scene, he clearly does not mean it. But in the powerful final moments of that episode, a member of his church is dying and needs her last rites administered before her final breath. A policeman tracks down Rev. Smallbone, takes him to the hospital, and asks him, "Are you her vicar?" Rev. Smallbone waffles. The policeman then asks repeatedly, "Are you her vicar?" Eventually, Rev. Smallbone quotes Isaiah 6: "Here I am, Lord. Send me." And he goes inside to be with the dying woman and her husband. Yes, he is still her vicar.

How do we know the plans God has for us? I really do not think we can or do. We know the plans we have for ourselves. We know those plans with certainty and clarity. But what about God's plans for us? That one is trickier. I have become less and less convinced that we can make (vocational) plans for ourselves, short- or long-term. I laugh when I hear a colleague say something like "I think I will be here for another four years, and then I'll go here and do this for ten years, then I will go here and do this." It is a never-ending cycle of trying to control the process and God's call.

All I really know is that I feel called to my current situation today. *In the here and now.* Then I will wake up tomorrow and see how it looks in the morning. Perhaps a healthy string of "yes" days means I am still called to be here, especially as I think about the ministry taking place and the ministry planned for the future and realize that I get excited. And then there are the other times when I think about the ministry at hand or down the road with pessimistic dread. This isn't me anymore. This is life-draining, not life-giving. During those times, I might find myself waking up day after day with a sense that God might be calling me somewhere else. Nevertheless, it isn't all based solely on the feelings that come about from one day to the next but continuous conversations. Sometimes we have to push through those hard days, and sometimes we might need to leave a place even if all is wonderful.

With Mihee being in ministry, it adds another layer to the stinky onion of discernment. Navigating two calls as husband and wife, and now as parents, is not easy. A lot gets juggled. Inevitably, sacrifices need to be made, and dreams need to be deferred. It can be hard. Real hard. I would be misleading you if I said that we have this thing figured out. But we have learned a few things along the way that might be worth passing along. For starters, ministry is a challenging vocation, not only because of the work involved but also because in every community there are only so many churches, let alone openings, let alone good fits, let alone two of them. We did not realize at the time how lucky we were while Mihee was serving her church in Pennsylvania and I was in New Jersey. We were about five miles apart. That is rare. I don't think you can expect to find that with every move and transition you make. Of course, that's not to say it doesn't happen, because it does every so often.

But ministry is challenging because a clergy cannot simply arrive in town and secure a job, or even assume there will be a job/call there for them anytime in the near future. We've learned that lesson. It is a specialized vocation, to be sure, but one that does not always present a lot of opportunities for two people at once (or at least opportunities that are close together). Another thing I have learned to remember is that before I was ever ordained to ministry, I was married to Mihee. Remembering the sacred calling of one's marriage, or a life together, is a holy act. In those vows we made promises no less sacred than we did at our ordination. And I honor those promises and those vows. So does Mihee. Sometimes that means one doesn't work in the field of choice. Vocational pride and goals can take some hits along the way. It takes a strong person to come to peace with that often hard reality. But that does not mean it has to be like that forever. We know God works in our lives in mysterious ways.

In the challenging waters of discerning our sense of call, I think we have found some peace in taking it day by day, month by month, and year by year. We let go of any grand, strategic, and elaborate plans to position ourselves where we think we want to end up. I've seen captains of those boats get capsized and thrown overboard into those choppy waters of discernment, perhaps ending up in the belly of a great fish (or whale) waiting to spit them out into whatever Nineveh God has in mind. Instead, we have learned time and time again that God is faithful, that God provides, that God is God, and that we are not. So when I am in those waters, I pray that I have the faith to simply take a deep breath, hold on tight—to God and to Mihee, for we are all three yoked together. As I do, I remember that we serve a God who says, "For surely I know the plans I have for you . . . plans for your welfare and not for harm, to give you a future with hope." Then I exhale and let go of everything else, and follow as hard as possible. Amen.

AFTERWORDS

Why is love beyond all measure of other human possibilities so rich and such a sweet burden for the one who has been struck by it? *Because we change ourselves into that which we love, and yet remain ourselves.* Then we would like to thank the beloved, but find nothing that would do it adequately. We can only be thankful to ourselves. Love transforms gratitude into faithfulness to ourselves and into an unconditional faith in the Other. Thus love steadily expands its most intimate secret. That the presence of the other breaks into our own life—this is what no feeling can fully encompass. Human fate gives itself to human fate, and it is the task of pure love to keep this self-surrender as vital as on the first day.

—Martin Heidegger[5]

We really have no idea what we are doing in this thing called life. Really. No. Clue.

Most days it feels like we are flying by the seat of our pants. Other days it feels like we have finally grown up, and we actually know something about ministry, budgets (both personal and church), and raising children (easy, when all they do is eat, sleep, and poop). Most of the time, though, I almost hear God's continuous chortle as we make plans, whether for the week or for the year, even for five years down the road. We now make loose plans, and look at them more as "goals" and "options." Like mile markers we just happened to come across. Now, it's less about the destination and so much more about the journey. Our churches taught us, and, yes, our kids and marriage have shown us, what our journey is meant to look like—we are called to "let go" and "give thanks." Surrender. Sanctification. When we do, we are certainly changed in so many ways, but we are used to not only transform but also make room for the Good.

—MKK

CONNECT

- In what ways do you express letting go? And giving thanks?
- Have you noticed any changes in your sense of call and/or hopes and dreams for ministry, as well as life? What were they five years ago? One year ago? What are they today? If there are shifts and changes, can you identify anything that has happened in your life that might explain why?
- Are there possibilities for ministry outside a formally validated ministry, and, if so, what? How can you support each other in these endeavors?

NOTES

INTRODUCTION

1. "Clergy Couple Counseling," the Archbishops' Council, accessed April 23, 2014, http://www.churchofengland.org/media/1168110/clergy%20couples%20guidance.pdf.

2. Dean Merrill, *Clergy Couples in Crisis: The Impact of Stress on Pastoral Marriages* (Nashville, TN: W Pub Group, 1986).

3. Reed Criswell and Elisabeth Staag, "Wedded to the Future: Clergy Couples Provide a New Paradigm for Leadership," *Divinity* (Duke Divinity School) 3, no. 2 (Winter 2004), accessed April 23, 2014, https://divinity.duke.edu/publications/2004.01/features/wedded/01.htm.

4. William Rabinor, "When Clergy Couples Come for Counseling," *Ministry* (July 2002). Rabinor's eight common issues among clergy couples are as follows: anger issues, marital gridlock, communication problems, loss of closeness, finances, dysfunctional behaviors, family issues, and marital "ghosts." By "ghost," he means spouses' inability to exorcise or forgive or let go of an issue that has haunted them from the past.

5. Donald G. Bloesch, *The Church: Sacraments, Worship, Ministry, Mission* (Downers Grove, IL: InterVarsity Press, 2002), 225.

6. Barbara Brown Zikmund, Adair T. Lummis, and Patricia Mei Yin Chang, *Clergy Women: An Uphill Calling* (Louisville, KY: Westminster John Knox Press, 1998), 42.

1. COLLISION

1. Lois K. Daly, *Feminist Theological Ethics: A Reader* (Louisville, KY: Westminster John Knox Press, 1994), 170.

2. Interview by Marianne Schnall, accessed April 20, 2014, http://www.gloriasteinem.com/qa/.

3. Serene Jones, *Feminist Theory and Christian Theology* (Minneapolis, MN: Augsburg Fortress, 2011), 22–23.

4. Seth Godin, "Stop Stealing Dreams," accessed April 18, 2014, http://sethgodin.typepad.com/stop_stealing_dreams/2012/03/stop-stealing-dreams-the-entire-manifesto-on-the-web-cleaned-up-html-version.html#section_19.

5. Oscar Wilde, *The Artist as Critic: Critical Writings of Oscar Wilde,* ed. Richard Ellmann (New York: Random House, 1969), 157.

6. Deborah Blagg and Susan Young, "What Makes a Good Leader," Harvard Business School, accessed April 20, 2014, https://www.alumni.hbs.edu/stories/Pages/story-bulletin.aspx?num=3059.

7. Oswald Chambers, *The Golden Book of Oswald Chambers: My Utmost for His Highest* (London: Simpkin, Marshall, 1934), 79.

2. CLOUT

1. Thomas McDonnell, "Hagia Sophia" in *A Thomas Merton Reader* (New York: Doubleday, 1989), 506.

2. Parker J. Palmer, *Let Your Life Speak* (San Francisco: Jossey-Bass, 2000), 12.

3. Virginia Satir, *The New Peoplemaking* (Mountain View, CA: Science and Behavior Books, 1988), 28.

4. Annie Dillard, "Living like Weasels" in *Encounters: Reading and the World*, eds. Pat C. Hoy II and Robert DiYanni (New York: McGraw, 1997), 211.

3. CHARISMA

1. Kahlil Gibran, *The Prophet* (New York: Knopf, 1955), 7.

2. "Occupy Wall Street," Wikipedia, accessed April 23, 2014, http://en.wikipedia.org/wiki/Occupy_wall_street.

3. Jack Kerouac, *On the Road* (New York: Viking, 1997), 5.

4. Mark 9:38.

5. Mark 9:39, 40.

4. CAUTION

1. M. Scott Peck, *Further Along the Road Less Travelled: Wisdom for the Journey towards Spiritual Growth* (London: Pocket, 2010), 1.

2. Martin B. Copenhaver and Lillian Daniel, *This Odd and Wondrous Calling: The Public and Private Lives of Two Ministers* (Grand Rapids, MI: Wm. B. Eerdmans, 2009).

3. Anne Linden, *Boundaries in Human Relationships: How to Be Separate and Connected* (Bancyfelin: Crown House, 2008), Location 378 of 2416 (Kindle).

4. Dietrich Bonhoeffer, *Life Together: The Classic Exploration of Faith in Community* (New York: Harper and Row, 1954), 26.

5. C. S. Lewis, *The Weight of Glory* (New York: HarperCollins, 1976), 22.

6. Frederick Buechner, *Telling Secrets* (San Francisco: HarperSanFrancisco, 1991), 2.

7. Buechner, *Telling*, 92.

8. Barbara Brown Taylor, *Leaving Church: A Memoir of Faith* (San Francisco: HarperSanFrancisco, 2006), 44.

5. COMBINATION

1. Neale Donald Walsch, *Conversations with God: An Uncommon Dialogue, Book 1* (New York: G. P. Putnam and Sons, 1996), 122–23.

2. Barbara Brown Taylor, *The Seeds of Heaven: Sermons on the Gospel of Matthew* (Louisville, KY: Westminster John Knox, 2004), 21.

3. Edward W. Said, *Orientalism* (New York: Vintage Books, 1979), 131.

4. Henri J. M. Nouwen, *Reaching Out: The Three Movements of the Spiritual Life* (Garden City, NY: Doubleday, 1975), 55.

5. Askhari Johnson Hodari and Yvonne McCalla Sobers, *Lifelines: The Black Book of Proverbs* (New York: Broadway Books, 2009), 42.

6. Rainer Maria Rilke, *Letters to a Young Poet*, trans. Joan M. Burnham (Novato, CA: New World Library, 2000), 9.

7. Charles Martin, *Thunder and Rain* (New York: Center Street, 2012), 269.

6. COOPERATION

1. Robert Burns, *Poems, Chiefly in the Scottish Dialect* (Kilmarnock: John Wilson, 1786), 138.

2. Betty Friedan, *The Feminine Mystique* (New York: Norton, 1963), 1.

3. "Primary Caregiver," Wikipedia, accessed April 20, 2014, http://en. wikipedia.org/wiki/Primary_caregiver.

4. Bonnie J. Miller-McLemore, *In the Midst of Chaos: Caring for Children as Spiritual Practice* (San Francisco: Jossey-Bass, 2009), chapter 5, section "Salvaging Sacrifice" (Kindle).

5. Ayelet Waldman, *Bad Mother: A Chronicle of Maternal Crimes, Minor Calamities, and Occasional Moments of Grace* (New York: Doubleday, 2009), 207.

6. Anne Lamott, *Operating Instructions: A Journal of My Son's First Year* (New York: Pantheon Books, 1993), May 31 journal entry.

7. "Abba's Child Quotes," Goodreads, accessed July 14, 2014, https://www. goodreads.com/work/quotes/513762-abba-s-child-the-cry-of-the-heart-for-intimate-belonging.

7. RE-CREATION

1. Walter Brueggemann, *Journey to the Common Good* (Louisville, KY: Westminster John Knox Press, 2010), 26.

2. "Buddhist Rest Day," Wikipedia, accessed April 23, 2014, http://en. wikipedia.org/wiki/Sabbath#Buddhist_rest_day.

3. Wayne Muller, *Sabbath: Finding Rest, Renewal, and Delight in Our Busy Lives* (New York: Bantam Books, 2000), 68.

4. May Sarton, *Journal of a Solitude* (New York: Norton, 1973).

5. Acts 2:41–47.

6. Barbara Brown Taylor, *An Altar in the World: A Geography of Faith* (New York: HarperCollins, 2009), 2.

7. Jonathan Safran Foer, "How Not to Be Alone," *New York Times*, June 8, 2013, accessed April 23, 2014, http://www.nytimes.com/2013/06/09/opinion/sunday/how-not-to-be-alone.html.

8. Muller, *Sabbath*, 6.

9. Maya Angelou, *Wouldn't Take Nothing for My Journey Now* (New York: Bantam Books, 1994), 138.

8. CHURCH ON SUNDAYS

1. Eugene H. Peterson, *The Pastor: A Memoir* (New York: HarperOne, 2011), 4.

2. Adapted from Psalm 19.

3. Oswald Chambers, *My Utmost for His Highest* (London: Simpkin, Marshall, 1934), 83.

4. John Calvin, *Institutes of the Christian Religion* (Philadelphia: Westminster Press, 1960), 16.

5. Marva J. Dawn, *Reaching Out without Dumbing Down: A Theology of Worship for the Turn-of-the-Century Culture* (Grand Rapids, MI: W. B. Eerdmans, 1995), 63.

6. N. T. Wright, *Simply Christian: Why Christianity Makes Sense* (San Francisco, CA: HarperSanFrancisco, 2006), 147.

9. COMMUNITY

1. C. S. Lewis, *The Four Loves* (New York: Harcourt Brace, 1960), 78.

2. A. A. Milne, *Walt Disney's Winnie the Pooh and Tigger too*, Grolier Book Club ed. (New York: Random House, 1975), 18.

3. Henri J. M. Nouwen, *The Road to Daybreak: A Spiritual Journey* (New York: Doubleday, 1988), 67.

4. David James Duncan, *God Laughs and Plays: Churchless Sermons in Response to the Preachments of the Fundamentalist Right* (Great Barrington, MA: Triad Institute, 2006), 136.

5. Mandy Zucker, "The 50 Best Quotes about Friendship," *Thought Catalog*, accessed April 20, 2014, http://thoughtcatalog.com/mandy-zucker/2013/10/50-quotes-about-friendship/.

10. CALLING

1. bell hooks and Cornel West, *Breaking Bread: Insurgent Black Intellectual Life* (Boston, MA: South End Press, 1991), 53.

2. Henri J. M. Nouwen, *Here and Now: Living in the Spirit* (New York: Crossroad, 1994), 6.

3. Madeleine L'Engle, *The Irrational Season* (New York: Seabury Press, 1977), 16.

4. Nouwen, *Here,* 24.

5. Martin Heidegger, *Being and Time* (New York: Harper, 1962), 288.

BIBLIOGRAPHY

Albom, Mitch. *The Five People You Meet in Heaven.* New York: Hyperion, 2003.

Angelou, Maya. *Wouldn't Take Nothing for My Journey Now.* New York: Bantam Books, 1994.

Atwood, Margaret. *The Blind Assassin.* New York: N. A. Talese, 2000.

Bloesch, Donald G. *The Church: Sacraments, Worship, Ministry, Mission.* Downers Grove, IL: InterVarsity Press, 2002.

Bonhoeffer, Dietrich. *Life Together: The Classic Exploration of Faith in Community.* New York: Harper and Row, 1954.

Brueggemann, Walter. *Journey to the Common Good.* Louisville, KY: Westminster John Knox Press, 2010.

Buechner, Frederick. *Telling Secrets.* San Francisco: HarperSanFrancisco, 1991.

Burns, Robert. *Poems, Chiefly in the Scottish Dialect.* Kilmarnock: John Wilson, 1786.

Calvin, John. *Institutes of the Christian Religion.* Philadelphia: Westminster Press, 1960.

Chambers, Oswald. *My Utmost for His Highest.* London: Simpkin, Marshall, 1934.

———. *The Golden Book of Oswald Chambers: My Utmost for His Highest.* London: Simpkin, Marshall, 1934.

Copenhaver, Martin B., and Lillian Daniel. *This Odd and Wondrous Calling: The Public and Private Lives of Two Ministers.* Grand Rapids, MI: Wm. B. Eerdmans, 2009.

Daly, Lois K. *Feminist Theological Ethics: A Reader.* Louisville, KY: Westminster John Knox Press, 1994.

Dawn, Marva J. *Reaching Out without Dumbing Down: A Theology of Worship for the Turn-of-the-Century Culture.* Grand Rapids, MI: W. B. Eerdmans, 1995.

Dillard, Annie. "Living like Weasels." In *Encounters: Reading and the World.* Editors Pat C. Hoy II and Robert DiYanni. New York: McGraw, 1997.

Duncan, David James. *God Laughs and Plays: Churchless Sermons in Response to the Preachments of the Fundamentalist Right.* Great Barrington, MA: Triad Institute, 2006.

Friedan, Betty. *The Feminine Mystique.* New York: Norton, 1963.

Gibran, Kahlil. *The Prophet.* New York: Knopf, 1955.

Heidegger, Martin. *Being and Time.* New York: Harper, 1962.

Hinckley, Marjorie Pay. *Small and Simple Things.* Salt Lake City: Deseret Books, 2003.

Hodari, Askhari Johnson, and Yvonne McCalla Sobers. *Lifelines: The Black Book of Proverbs.* New York: Broadway Books, 2009.

hooks, bell, and Cornel West. *Breaking Bread: Insurgent Black Intellectual Life.* Boston, MA: South End Press, 1991.

Jones, Serene. *Feminist Theory and Christian Theology.* Minneapolis, MN: Augsburg Fortress, 2011.

Kerouac, Jack. *On the Road*. New York: Viking, 1997.

L'Engle, Madeleine. *The Irrational Season*. New York: Seabury Press, 1977.

Lamott, Anne. *Operating Instructions: A Journal of My Son's First Year*. New York: Pantheon Books, 1993.

Lewis, C. S. *The Four Loves*. New York: Harcourt Brace, 1960.

———. *The Collected Letters of C. S. Lewis, Volume 3: Narnia, Cambridge, and Joy, 1950–1963*, ed. Walter Hooper. San Francisco: HarperSanFrancisco, 2007.

———. *The Weight of Glory*. New York: HarperCollins, 1976.

Linden, Anne. *Boundaries in Human Relationships: How to Be Separate and Connected*. Bancyfelin: Crown House, 2008.

Martin, Charles. *Thunder and Rain*. New York: Center Street, 2012.

McDonnell, Thomas. "Hagia Sophia" in *A Thomas Merton Reader*. New York: Doubleday, 1989.

Merrill, Dean. *Clergy Couples in Crisis: The Impact of Stress on Pastoral Marriages*. Nashville, TN: W Pub Group, 1986.

Merton, Thomas. *The Way of Chuang-Tzu*. New York: New Directions, 1965.

Miller-McLemore, Bonnie J. *In the Midst of Chaos: Caring for Children as Spiritual Practice*. San Francisco: Jossey-Bass, 2009.

Milne, A. A. *Walt Disney's Winnie the Pooh and Tigger Too*. Grolier Book Club edition. New York: Random House, 1975.

Muller, Wayne. *Sabbath: Finding Rest, Renewal, and Delight in Our Daily Lives*. New York: Bantam Books, 2000.

Nouwen, Henri J. M. *Reaching Out: The Three Movements of the Spiritual Life*. Garden City, NY: Doubleday, 1975.

———. *Here and Now: Living in the Spirit*. New York: Crossroad, 1994.

———. *The Road to Daybreak: A Spiritual Journey*. New York: Doubleday, 1988.

Palmer, Parker J. *Let Your Life Speak*. San Francisco: Jossey-Bass, 2000.

Peck, M. Scott. *Further Along the Road Less Travelled: Wisdom for the Journey towards Spiritual Growth*. London: Pocket, 2010.

Peterson, Eugene H. *The Pastor: A Memoir*. New York: HarperOne, 2011.

Picoult, Jodi. *My Sister's Keeper*. New York: Atria Books, 2004.

Rabinor, William. "When Clergy Couples Come for Counseling," *Ministry*, July 2002.

Rilke, Rainer Maria. *Letters to a Young Poet*. Translator Joan M. Burnham. Novato, CA: New World Library, 2000.

Said, Edward W. *Orientalism*. New York: Vintage Books, 1979.

Sarton, May. *Journal of a Solitude*. New York: Norton, 1973.

Satir, Virginia. *The New Peoplemaking*. Mountain View, CA: Science and Behavior Books, 1988.

Sparks, Nicholas. *The Wedding*. New York: Warner Books, 2003.

Swindoll, Charles R. *Jesus: The Greatest Life of All*. Nashville: Thomas Nelson, 2008.

Taylor, Barbara Brown. *An Altar in the World: A Geography of Faith*. New York: HarperCollins, 2009.

———. *Leaving Church: A Memoir of Faith*. San Francisco: HarperSanFrancisco, 2006.

———. *The Seeds of Heaven: Sermons on the Gospel of Matthew*. Louisville, KY: Westminster John Knox, 2004.

Waldman, Ayelet. *Bad Mother: A Chronicle of Maternal Crimes, Minor Calamities, and Occasional Moments of Grace*. New York: Doubleday, 2009.

Walsch, Neale Donald. *Conversations with God: An Uncommon Dialogue, Book 1*. New York: G. P. Putnam and Sons, 1996.

Wilde, Oscar. *The Artist as Critic: Critical Writings of Oscar Wilde*. Edited by Richard Ellmann. New York: Random House, 1969.

Wright, N. T. *Simply Christian: Why Christianity Makes Sense*. San Francisco, CA: HarperSanFrancisco, 2006.

Zikmund, Barbara Brown, Adair T. Lummis, and Patricia Mei Yin Chang. *Clergy Women: An Uphill Calling*. Louisville, KY: Westminster John Knox Press, 1998.